Cambridge Elements ☰

Elements in Epistemology
edited by
Stephen Hetherington
University of New South Wales, Sydney

THE *A PRIORI* WITHOUT MAGIC

Jared Warren
Stanford University, California

CAMBRIDGE
UNIVERSITY PRESS

CAMBRIDGE
UNIVERSITY PRESS

Shaftesbury Road, Cambridge CB2 8EA, United Kingdom

One Liberty Plaza, 20th Floor, New York, NY 10006, USA

477 Williamstown Road, Port Melbourne, VIC 3207, Australia

314–321, 3rd Floor, Plot 3, Splendor Forum, Jasola District Centre,
New Delhi – 110025, India

103 Penang Road, #05–06/07, Visioncrest Commercial, Singapore 238467

Cambridge University Press is part of Cambridge University Press & Assessment,
a department of the University of Cambridge.

We share the University's mission to contribute to society through the pursuit of
education, learning and research at the highest international levels of excellence.

www.cambridge.org
Information on this title: www.cambridge.org/9781009015769
DOI: 10.1017/9781009030472

First published 2022

A catalogue record for this publication is available from the British Library.

ISBN 978-1-009-01576-9 Paperback
ISSN 2398-0567 (online)
ISSN 2514-3832 (print)

The *A Priori* Without Magic

Elements in Epistemology

DOI: 10.1017/9781009030472
First published online: September 2022

Jared Warren
Stanford University, California
Author for correspondence: Jared Warren, jaredwar@stanford.edu

Abstract: The distinction between the *a priori* and the *a posteriori* is an old and influential one. But both the distinction itself and the crucial notion of *a priori* knowledge face powerful philosophical challenges. Many philosophers worry that accepting the *a priori* is tantamount to accepting epistemic magic. In contrast, this Element argues that the *a priori* can be formulated clearly, made respectable, and used to do important epistemological work. The author's conception of the *a priori* and its role falls short of what some historical proponents of the notion may have hoped for, but it allows us to accept and use the notion without abandoning either naturalism or empiricism, broadly understood. This Element argues that we can accept and use the *a priori* without magic.

Keywords: *a priori*, epistemology, inferentialism, rationalism, naturalism, conventionalism, meaning-based theory of the *a priori*

ISBNs: 9781009015769 (PB), 9781009030472 (OC)
ISSNs: 2398-0567 (online), 2514-3832 (print)

Contents

Preface

On November 1, 2020, Stephen Hetherington wrote to me asking if I'd like to submit a proposal for a Cambridge Elements volume on the *a priori* to appear in the epistemology series he was editing. I had no standing interest in contributing to a book series, but Stephen's vision for the Elements volumes under his editorship appealed to me – short, elegantly written, accessible without being a survey, and actually *saying something*.

This called to mind two books, both titled *Philosophy of Logic*, one by Quine, the other by Putnam. Both are accessible without being introductory surveys and both were written for a book series – Quine's for the Beardsleys' Foundations of Philosophy series and Putnam's for Danto's Harper Essays in Philosophy series. Both books also managed to succeed on all of Stephen's *desiderata*. The thought of trying to do as well appealed to me. So I agreed; my proposal was submitted on November 30 and accepted soon after.

If you are only interested in money or acclaim then writing a serious philosophy book is a waste of time. After your book falls dead-born from the press, you're either rewarded with total silence or subjected to a handful of academic book "reviews." Given this, it can be difficult to muster the effort of will required. To manage it, the writing process must be its own reward. You must enjoy losing yourself in a philosophical topic. So, more than anything else, a desire to better understand the *a priori* was my motivation for writing this Element.

I had already thought and written quite a bit about the *a priori* when I submitted my proposal. My first book, *Shadows of Syntax*, gives an inferentialist-conventionalist theory of logic and mathematics that upholds the *a priori* status of both disciplines. But only one chapter in that book (chapter 6) is solely focused on epistemology, and though I was already well read on the *a priori*, I had never done a sustained deep dive into the literature on the topic.

I tend to get obsessed with philosophical issues. This sometimes results in wonderful stretches of time during which I do very little but read and think about the topic constantly. It's a bit like being in love, including the risk of heartbreak. I had previously delved into conditionals, rule following, the liar paradox, grue, and a few other topics in this hyper-focused fashion. My original plan was to steep myself in the *a priori* starting early in 2021, but that plan was derailed, initially by an inability to put a pause on my liar-paradox obsession, and then by a crisis.

My focused *a priori* research was ultimately delayed until the fall and winter of 2021. Despite my previous familiarity with much of the *a priori* literature, I learned a lot from and was enriched by the experience. This Element was submitted for review at the end of January 2022; a post-review version was submitted in early April and officially accepted in early June, a polished version was submitted for production in mid-June. Proofs were corrected in late July.

Though short and (I hope) accessible, this Element aims to contribute to our understanding of the *a priori* in a variety of ways and to stake out and defend a sophisticated, meaning-based approach to *a priori* warrant.

With no magic.

Palo Alto, California

Introduction

There is a natural, felt difference between beliefs that are rooted in experience and beliefs that are not. This difference is enshrined in the traditional distinction between the *a priori* and the *a posteriori* in epistemology.

Once upon a time, many philosophers believed that some substantive claims about the world could be known *a priori*. These facts about objective reality were there for the epistemic taking, no matter your particular life experiences. According to this once common thought, humans could make discoveries about the world without ever leaving their armchairs. Having been given this hammer, almost every fact started to look like a nail. Not only the origin of reality, not only the existence of God, not only the nature of God, but much, much else besides was "proved" *a priori* by eager philosophers.

In retrospect, a lot of this was absurd – so absurd that it's now natural to be skeptical about the *a priori* as a category. Though natural, this is an overreaction. Some facts *are* accessible from the armchair. Rather than banishing the *a priori*, we should tame and demystify it. When shorn of overreach, the *a priori/a posteriori* distinction remains a useful epistemological division. It is well-worth keeping in our conceptual tool kit, provided we realize that nails suitable for this hammer are relatively few.

This point of view isn't often expressed out loud, but I think it's quite common. While I was writing this Element, the results of an extensive 2020 survey of philosophers' beliefs were released on www.philpapers.org. According to this survey, over 70 percent of philosophers accept or lean toward accepting *a priori* knowledge, with under 20 percent rejecting it. And around 30 percent of philosophers accept or lean toward the old rationalist ways of thinking that originally gave the *a priori* a bad reputation. It seems that many philosophers still accept the *a priori* while rejecting magic.

This Element clarifies the concept of the *a priori*, criticizes magical theories, and offers a simple, non-magical theory of the *a priori* that dovetails with what naturalistically minded philosophers actually think deep down in their heart of hearts.

1 Epistemic Evaluation

Cognitive systems like us have various beliefs. For a small personal selection: I believe that two is an even number, that all politicians are wicked, and that this Element will be a surprise *New York Times* best seller.

Most of us now accept a broadly scientific, broadly naturalistic picture of the mind and the world. According to this picture, human cognition results – somehow, someway – from the physical operation of the embodied brain. An interdisciplinary science may eventually be able to tell us exactly how each of our beliefs came into existence. Yet even now an inexact but broadly accurate account is possible. Our beliefs are formed using a motley of methods and in a variety of ways, but all of these methods and ways are causal processes, broadly speaking.

This is much, but it is not enough. In addition to *describing* processes of belief formation and the beliefs they give rise to, we also *evaluate* them. For better or worse, this is where philosophy enters the scene. It must, for evaluating differs from describing; you can't get an "ought" from an "is." When we evaluate beliefs and belief-forming methods, as opposed to merely describing them, we are doing epistemology, not science. In epistemology we both make and theorize about epistemic evaluations.

Epistemic evaluation ultimately concerns distinctive epistemic norms. Is it *appropriate* for us to form beliefs using a particular method? Given our evidence, *should* we believe this claim? *Must* we believe it? I have used neutral normative terminology here, but epistemic evaluations are usually made with distinctive epistemic terminology. As we'll see, this terminological thicket is quite tangled.

Of course, there are also non-epistemic ways to evaluate beliefs. Many humanities professors think the belief that there are intelligence differences between human races is immoral. Perhaps so, but this is to condemn the belief in *moral* but not epistemic terms. Positive psychologists will tell you the belief that you are untalented bodes ill for your future prospects. Perhaps so, but this is to condemn the belief in *practical* but not epistemic terms. Epistemic evaluations need not align with either moral or practical evaluations. Our evidence might give us an epistemic obligation to believe something that is both morally and practically ill-advised. Some would dispute this. At the very least though, connections between distinct evaluative practices must be argued for, not simply assumed.

I mentioned earlier that epistemic evaluations typically employ distinctive terminology. The most familiar bit of epistemological terminology is "knowledge" and its cognates – the word "epistemology" itself partly derives from the Greek word for knowledge, "episteme." Knowing something, as opposed to merely believing it, is an exalted epistemic status. As this way of talking suggests, knowledge requires belief. If you don't believe that all politicians are wicked, then you don't know it either. This is relatively uncontroversial. It is also relatively uncontroversial that knowledge requires truth. If something isn't true, then it can't be known. Popular challenges to this platitude confuse the epistemic notion of knowledge with the psychological notion of certainty. This is a mistake. Being certain about something isn't the same thing as knowing it. As life soon teaches us all, certainty does not guarantee truth. Nor are we psychologically certain of everything we know.

Almost everything else about knowledge is controversial. It is controversial, for example, whether knowledge requires justification. All agree that lucky guesses don't count as knowledge, but it's unclear whether having justification for a belief is the key differentiating feature. Once upon a time though, many philosophers thought that knowing was the same thing as having a justified, true belief. According to this analysis, I know that my dog Chrysippus is in the backyard just in case I have a justified true belief that Chrysippus is in the backyard. This is the justified-true-belief analysis of knowledge. The analysis is neat, tidy, aesthetically pleasing, and wrong.

This is shown by cases where a justified belief is true by accident. In these cases, the believer gets lucky. Through the kitchen window I see the back door open and hear a dog's bark coming from the backyard. Based on these experiences, I believe that Chrysippus is in the backyard. This belief is justified. It's also true, for in fact, Chrysippus *is* in the backyard. However, the dog I heard was the neighbor's dog. Also, Chrysippus didn't get out through the open back door, but instead by going out the front door and digging under the backyard fence. I have a justified true belief that Chrysippus is in the backyard, but it's not knowledge. Examples like this are called "Gettier cases."[1]

Accidental correctness is incompatible with knowing. And Gettier cases show that being justified doesn't screen out every kind of accidental correctness. In response, most philosophers have concluded that a nontrivial analysis of knowledge requires an additional condition ruling out the luck illustrated in Gettier cases. Many – *many* – different proposals have been offered.[2] An alternative approach drops the attempted analysis and characterizes knowledge directly with an anti-accident condition.[3]

Despite this, most philosophers still think that something like justification is the central notion of pure epistemic evaluation. In matters of pure epistemic goodness, it is the coin of the realm. But as often happens in philosophy, terminology is not standard. In addition to "justified" and its cognates, you will also find "warranted," "rational," "reasonable," "entitled," and more. Adding to the

---

[1] From Gettier (1963).
[2] For an overview of the first decade of this research, see Shope (1983).
[3] This need not be offered as part of a definition of "knowledge"; see Williamson (2000).

confusion, these terms are often used for related but distinct notions. This is possible because our ordinary practices of epistemic evaluation have several distinct but intertwined strands. Let me tease some of these strands apart before setting out my own preferred terminology. Three distinctions are of particular importance.

The first is between having some epistemic goodness and reaching a threshold level of epistemic goodness. René has *some justification for* thinking that Chrysippus will bite him, but that doesn't mean he is *justified in* thinking that Chrysippus will bite him. The threshold notion concerns whether it is epistemically appropriate to have the belief, all things considered. Most epistemic terms witness this dichotomy.

"some justification for" versus "justified"
"some reason for" versus "reasonable"
"some warrant for" versus "warranted"

The terms "reasonable" and "rational" well serve this notion, but they can apply without evidence. This distinction is crucial, since there is a conceptual possibility that some of our beliefs meet the threshold without any positive backing. Our terminology shouldn't rule this out without comment.

The second crucial distinction notes that terms for epistemic goodness, though most often applied to beliefs, can also be applied to belief-forming methods. We might be justified in forming beliefs by way of inference, or based on perception, or with appeals to memory; but not justified in forming beliefs via coin flip or by consulting a psychic. Of course, to say that we are justified in forming beliefs via inference does not mean that every inference rule can justifiably be used. Forming new beliefs using the rule of *modus ponens* is justified but forming beliefs using the rule of affirming the consequent is not. When we say that someone is justified in forming beliefs by way of inference, this is a shorthand way of saying that they are justified in using certain inference rules. In the discussion to follow, I will consider the epistemic status of beliefs, general methods of belief formation, and specific inference rules.

The third and final crucial distinction concerns what is, broadly speaking, *inside of* versus what is *outside of* a believer. Nonphilosophers like René form beliefs using perception. So-formed, René's beliefs are in epistemic good standing. Some think that this is entirely owed to facts internal to René – his mental states, or perhaps only his accessible mental states. Others disagree, thinking instead that the good standing of René's perceptual beliefs also depends on the external situation René is operating in. Call the first group *internalists*, the second *externalists*. The traditional epistemological project assumed a strong form of internalism.

According to this view, justification requires at least the possibility of first-person cognitive access. More recently both externalism and less-demanding forms of internalism have become more and more popular. I think we should split the difference. Our everyday practices of epistemic evaluation include *both* externalist and internalist elements, so there is little wisdom in opting for one over the other, up front. We should include terms for both externalist and internalist kinds of epistemic goodness in our tool kit, while also having a neutral covering term.

Before explicitly setting out my own terminology, I want to bring up two more distinctions. These are important in epistemology but won't be of much concern in this Element. I mention them only to set them aside without any lingering confusions.

First, you might have noticed that we sometimes talk about epistemic goodness as something that can be measured and at other times as something that can be counted. René has *some justification for* thinking Chrysippus will bite him just in case he has *a justification for* thinking Chrysippus will bite him. Most terms for epistemic goodness witness this dichotomy:

> "some justification for" versus "a justification for"
> "some reason for" versus "a reason for"
> "some warrant for" versus "a warrant for"

The term "evidence" does too but also seems slightly narrower in excluding some reasons for believing (proofs, intuition). Both ways of talking allow us to discuss justification either for or against particular claims. We usually toggle between the two ways of talking easily, using whichever is most natural for the case at hand. I won't mark any substantive distinction between them here.

Second, some philosophers think epistemic evaluations are context-sensitive. What counts as "knowledge" in one context may not so-count in a different context, likewise for justification. In everyday contexts, René knows that he has hands on the basis of perception. When sitting in his skepticism class, he does not, for if he did, he would also know that he is not a brain in a vat on the basis of perception, which he does not. Sometimes distinctions are also made between different types of context-sensitivity, but I won't be concerned with this here. We can remain fairly noncommittal while admitting that epistemic evaluations may well be sensitive to context (or interests) in a number of different ways. With all of these distinctions now noted, you can see what I meant about the terminological tangle.

To cut a path through the tangle, I'll use the term "warrant" and its cognates for the neutral notion of epistemic goodness. I'll allow it to apply to beliefs, methods, and rules. I will use "entitlement" for specifically externalist warrant, and "justification" for specifically internalist warrant (see Figure 1).[4]

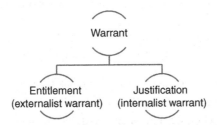

Figure 1 The relationship between warrant, entitlement, and justification

I allow that entitlements can be automatic or earned, in an externalist sense of "earned." We can think of this in analogy to rights. Just like other rights, epistemic rights can be automatic or earned. René has an automatic right to freedom of speech, but only has a right to speak for his town after being elected mayor. Epistemic entitlements, whether automatic or earned, contrast with justifications. Justification can come from evidence, but it might also be generated in other ways – through discovering a proof, or being in a particular mental state. As far as possible, I will remain neutral about the *exact* nature of both entitlement and justification.

When I say that René's belief is *warranted*, I am saying that René belief is epistemically appropriate in the relevant context. If it is not warranted, the belief is epistemically inappropriate. The threshold is met by having enough warrant, in the relevant context. When I say that René has *a warrant*, or has *some warrant*, I am saying that René has either entitlement or justification or both, in that context. The connection to the standards of a context will usually be left implicit.

In setting things up in this way, I am not assuming that any epistemic entitlements actually are automatic; I am merely allowing that as an option. Later I will argue that some entitlements are automatic, but someone who rejects this can freely adopt my terminology. A true belief being warranted is not sufficient for knowledge, due to the aforementioned Gettier cases.[5] We should also allow, in principle, that warrant is fallible. You can have warrant for a belief that turns out to be false, at least as far as my terminology is concerned. In fact, my terminology is neutral on the important epistemological questions. The essential thing is to be clear about how terms are being used, so that others can translate my claims into their own favored ways of talking.

Our central question can now be stated: *does all epistemic warrant depend on experience?* Warrant that does not depend on experience is *a priori*, warrant that

---

[4] The term "entitlement" was introduced with roughly this usage in Burge (1993).
[5] Plantinga (1993) used "warrant" as a term for whatever differentiated true belief from knowledge, but this usage differs from mine.

does depend on experience is *a posteriori*. If there is entitlement or justification that does not depend on experience, there is *a priori* warrant. If there is not, the *a priori* is empty. To make progress, we need a detailed characterization of *a priority*.[6]

2 Characterizing the *A Priori*

There is a natural distinction between warrant that depends on sense experience or empirical evidence and warrant that does not. Something like this distinction was recognized in scholastic philosophy and thereby made its way into early modern philosophy in the work of Descartes, Leibniz, Berkeley, and others. Both the distinction and the "*a priori*" versus "*a posteriori*" terminology for it were cemented for all time in Kant's byzantine masterpiece, 1781's *Critique of Pure Reason*.

We can use the base notion of *a priori* warrant to characterize derivative notions of *a priori* knowledge and truth:

> Something is *a priori* knowledge for someone just in case they know it on the basis of *a priori* warrant

This should be understood as ruling out cases where you have warrant but don't base your beliefs on it – I find a mathematical proof of a claim, but decline to believe it on the basis of my proof and instead believe it because Unreliable Andy told me it was true. Believing a claim on the basis of *a priori* warrant is usually believing it by way of a method that confers *a priori* warrant.

Characterizing *a priori* truth is more difficult. We could say that for each individual the truths they know *a priori* are their personal *a priori* truths. We could say that, but we won't. It isn't what philosophers mean when they call something an "*a priori* truth." They instead intend a classification among the truths that doesn't vary from person to person. To capture this we need a different approach. Suppose we say:

> Something is an *a priori* truth just in case it can be known by someone, in some context, *a priori* (truths that are not *a priori* are *a posteriori*)[7]

---

[6] Sometimes "*a prioricity*" is used instead of "*a priority*," but this is a linguistic mistake based on an analogy with "analyticity"; see the opening note to Burge (2000), where Burge mentions learning this from Quine. This was at the 1993 Rutgers summer institute on the nature of meaning, at which Quine was visibly wincing at the term "*a prioricity*." Some attendees thought Quine was pained by the mere use of any term for his hated notion, but his pain was owed to the language, not the philosophy. Thanks to Dave Chalmers for relaying this story.

[7] A lengthy discussion of truth-bearers was excised for space. To remain neutral, I usually use "claim" instead of "sentence," "proposition," or "statement." Clarity about these differences is crucial at several points later in the text, especially in Sections 5 and 7.

We need to understand the "can" here so that, so-characterized, the *a priori* "truths" are *actually true*. You can't know something that isn't true. As long as the "can" means something like, "it is possible in our world or in a nearby world with the same (relevant) truths," then the *a priori* "truths" so-characterized really will be true.

Still, it isn't exactly clear when something "can be known by someone, in some context, *a priori*." Some religious scholars have claimed that God automatically knows absolutely everything. Does this mean that "someone," namely God, can know absolutely everything *a priori*? If so, this characterization turns every single truth into an *a priori* truth, defeating the entire point.

We can best avoid this by focusing on belief-forming methods. Some belief-forming methods produce *a priori* warrant, others do not. We can explain the right-hand-side of this characterization of *a priori* truth by appealing to methods. An *a priori* truth is a truth that can be known in an *a priori* way – that is, by using a belief-forming method that confers *a priori* warrant. Which methods are these? We could simply list the *a priori* methods, one by one, but that isn't very satisfying. It would be better to have a general characterization of *a priori* warrant that allows us to classify novel belief-forming methods should we encounter them.[8]

Martians or robots might be very different from humans. They might have very different brains or no brains at all. Despite this, they might still form beliefs on the basis of sensory experiences. This is possible even if their senses differ from ours in power or in kind. Mundane examples prove the same point. When bats form beliefs about their local, external environment on the basis of echo-location, they are still forming beliefs using sensory experience, even though the sense they are using is one that humans lack entirely (or, at best, have only in a very poor form). Even alien belief-forming methods can be classified using our notions.

In the God example, God knows everything automatically. This is not a belief-forming method at all, since belief *formation* requires a state change. You start without the belief in question and then form (and possibly maintain) the belief using a particular method and thereafter have the belief. This doesn't apply to an omniscient God. Because of this, it is a distortion to think of God's "method" as perception or introspection on steroids. Instead, God just has every true belief, innately. The next section will argue that innate beliefs can be *a priori*, but only in a situated way that needs to be set aside when characterizing *a priori* truth.

For these reasons, a better characterization of *a priori* truth is as follows:

---

[8] Compare Williamson (2013) on "bottom-up" versus "top-down" characterizations of the *a priori*.

Something is an *a priori* truth just in case it can be known by someone, in some context, using (only) a belief-forming method that confers *a priori* warrant.

In most cases that we can describe, it will be clear which belief-forming method is being used, and we will be able to evaluate and classify the method, often by noticing relevant similarities between it and our own belief-forming methods. Similarity is always a bit fuzzy and context-sensitive, but the lingering fuzziness here is harmless.

This characterization allows us to say that something is an *a priori* truth even when we don't, ourselves, have *a priori* warrant for believing it. I believe that Fermat's Last Theorem is true because I know the famous story about Andrew Wiles proving it. However, I have not worked through the proof myself, and have only a dim idea of how it goes. Still, Fermat's Last Theorem is an *a priori* truth because a non-magical belief-forming method – mathematical proof – used by beings with non-magical cognitive capacities – Andrew Wiles among them – can produce *a priori* warrant sufficient for knowing it, given the factual situation.

The distinction between *a priori* and *a posteriori* truth is difficult to perfectly isolate historically. This is because there are several other distinctions that largely overlap with it in how they classify cases. In particular, consider the following two distinctions between different kinds of truths:

necessary truths (could not be otherwise) versus contingent truths (could have been otherwise)

analytic truths (true in virtue of meaning alone) versus synthetic truths (true in virtue of meaning together with the facts)

Empiricists used to argue that these three distinctions perfectly line up. This view is not so popular now, as challenges from Kripke and others have put extreme pressure on it.[9] I will revisit this issue in Sections 5 and 6. Here I simply note for the record that I am not assuming anything up front about the relationship between *a priori*, necessary, and analytic truths.

The discussion so far shows that we can make sense of *a priori* knowledge and truth, *provided that* we can make sense of the base notion of *a priori* warrant. This, as they say, is where the action is. But the very idea of *a priori* warrant is *prima facie* puzzling. How can beings like us, physical creatures in a physical world, gain any warrant except through experience? All of our methods for investigating the world essentially involve experience.

---

[9] In Kripke (1980).

I already noted that we could just stipulate that some methods – mathematical proof, armchair reasoning – confer *a priori* warrant and be done. This approach is sometimes useful when classifying cases, but it tells us nothing about what is distinctive of the *a priori*. Without a general characterization, it's natural to wonder whether there is anything unified about the category. Fortunately there is a standard characterization going back – at least – to Kant:

a priori warrant is warrant that is independent of experience

This is usually understood with a built-in explanatory direction: *a priori* warrant for believing something is *a priori* because it is independent of experience. Being independent of experience is why some warrant is *a priori*, as opposed to *a posteriori*. If anything unifies the category of the *a priori*, it is this. The concept of the *a priori* is the concept of epistemic goodness that is not owed to experience.

This is an advance, but it is still a bit schematic. The standard characterization uses two terms – "experience" and "independent" – that call out for elaboration. Let's provide this elaboration, starting with "experience." Sometimes characterizations of the *a priori* instead talk about "empirical evidence." This is a difference of terminology, not of doctrine – empirical evidence is, by definition, the evidence of experience. There is no way to get around it; we need some characterization of "experience" to understand the *a priori*.

In colloquial speech, people sometimes use "experience" to pick out *any* phenomenal state over some given time. This is not the sense of the term we need.[10] The meaning of "experience" that matters here concerns online sensory processing of a special kind. More particularly, aspects of sensory states that are caused by the world. This includes both states caused by the external world and states caused by the internal world – having a headache and being hungry should count as "experiences," in the relevant sense. As it stands, this is a bit rough and ready. Albert Casullo has argued that "experience" in this needed sense is a natural kind term.[11] I wouldn't say that, exactly, but even if it's right, we need more detail about this concept of experience.

Here is a brief account of how we build, from the inside, to the realization that not all deliverances of our senses count as "experiences." Humans have various senses, primarily the canonical "five senses" – sight, hearing, smell, taste, and touch. Most would add to this list, but we don't need a full taxonomy here. Our senses operate causally, giving us information about the local features of the physical world, externally or internally. We can think of each of our senses as complex systems that are in particular states at particular times, so that the

---

[10] Casullo (2003) also makes this point.   [11] In section 6.2 of Casullo (2003).

accessible states of all of your senses at a given time constitute your overall sensory state at that given time. Call a continuous, unbroken sequence of these overall sensory states over a stretch of time a sensory run. Sometimes, during a sensory run, some of the deliverances of the senses, together, in sequence, constitute an experience. Not always though. A period of sitting around with your eyes closed thinking about a mathematical proof and nothing else involves a sensory run but no experience. The difficulty is in saying what distinguishes the experiential features from the non-experiential features of a sensory run.

This problem was implicitly posed in early modern philosophy. The pre-Kantian modern philosophers accepted a theory of mind according to which mental operations consisted of nothing but accessible sensory states and their components. These components were often called "ideas," though terminology wasn't uniform.[12] There is *something* right about this, but the focus on immediate sensory experiences led the early moderns into a fundamental muddle. The muddle was a tendency to directly identify meanings and concepts with the *local* properties of particular sensory experiences. In the extreme, this involved identifying concepts themselves with mental particulars of a sensory nature. On one version of this view, the concept of a horse *is* a generic mental image of a horse. This is a deep distortion. A far better picture emerged subsequently, when philosophers began to explain meanings and concepts in terms of clusters of dispositions and abilities.

Despite the distortion, the early moderns helpfully appealed to several dimensions along which sensory runs could be distinguished. Let me list a few of these dimensions, along with an early modern philosopher who focused on it:

> Clarity (Descartes)
> Detail (Locke)
> Vividness (Hume)
> Involuntariness (Berkeley)

Some accessible states of our sensory systems (including component states) have clarity, detail, and vividness that other such states lack. These are differences of degree, of course. They are also distinct features, but as a matter of fact, they tend to cluster together. In addition, some of our sensory states are under our control while others are not. When I look out of my window, my will does not control the activation of my sensory system. Yet when I imagine a pink elephant upon explicit instruction, it does. As a matter of empirical fact, it tends to be the case that the clearest, most detailed, and most vivid sensory states are

---

[12] See Bennett (1966).

also the ones that are entirely outside of my volitional control. This is the key point that initially distinguishes the experiential aspects of a sensory run from other aspects, such as those involved in imagination.

There are a couple of obvious hiccups. What about dreams? Sensory runs during dreams are not under our control, but this isn't a serious problem. Those sensory runs also lack clarity, detail, and vividness.[13] Do dreams count as experiences? This has been debated, but it's a verbal issue.[14] We need to distinguish dream "experiences" from normal, waking experiences, whether or not we call both "experiences." The features I've noted allow us to do this. The dream "experiences" are among those that, while involuntary, also lack in clarity, detail, and vividness.

Another worry concerns exactly what is meant by calling a sensory run "involuntary." We can almost always exercise *some* measure of voluntary control over the light show in our heads by controlling what we are attending to. Despite this, there remains a clear difference between those qualitative features that are produced voluntarily and those that are not. We can admit this while also admitting that humans can direct their attention in ways that allow different qualitative features to be recognized, noticed, and understood over involuntarily produced qualitative states.

Summing all of this up, we can say the following:

A *prima facie* experience consists of all aspects of a sensory run that are clear, detailed, and vivid, while also being involuntarily.

This provides a *prima facie* concept of experience that is drawn entirely from the inside. The *prima facie* notion then gives rise to a settled notion. The settled notion comes from the realization that the continuities and patterns in *prima facie* experiences call out for explanation. We start with the *prima facie* notion, drawn in terms of qualitative meta-features of sensory states and their relation to what used to be called "the will." We then refine this concept, eventually positing an independent world to explain both the generation of *prima facie* experiences and the existence of sensory capacities altogether.

I also think that we are rational in positing an independent external world partly on this basis, but that is not the claim I'm making at the moment.[15] I am only making a descriptive claim that *we do* posit an independent external world partly on the basis of experience, so understood.[16]

---

[13] See Leite (2011) for discussion and citation of empirical evidence for this and related claims.

[14] For example, see Dennett (1976).

[15] This would be an abductive or "inference to the best explanation" reply to external world skepticism; see Beebe (2009) for an overview.

[16] The descriptive claim was perhaps first made in detail by Hume; see Bennett (1971) and Price (1940).

Ultimately this process leads us back to our initial, naive, characterization:

> An experience consists of all aspects of a sensory run that are produced by the
> world in a relevant involuntary fashion.

This concept of experience is foundational to our conceptual scheme. We didn't start here, conceptually, but there is a route, from the inside, via the *prima facie* notion of an experience to this settled notion. The route from there to here involves an iterated feedback process. Our final, settled concept of experience is the outcome of this feedback process. At the end, we are easily able to count some unclear sensory runs – such as the drunkard's, those we have in poor lighting, and so on – as *experiences*, all the same. The best explanation of the lack of clarity in those cases is *not* that the relevant aspects didn't issue from the external world.

I think Casullo is driven to call this a "natural kind" concept because we aren't simply defining "experience" and then holding fast to our definition. We instead revise our understanding in response to feedback from the world. I agree, but I prefer to classify it as a *theoretical* concept. I also don't think much hangs on this point of terminology. I intend my account of "experience" to be both descriptively plausible and also neutral on the controversial philosophical debates in the vicinity.[17] Further details could be added, but enough has been said to clarify one aspect of the standard characterization of the a priori. We still need to understand "independence." With this term, things won't be quite so unified.

The first obvious idea is that dependence is *causal*. Some beliefs are caused by experience, and others aren't. The second obvious idea is that dependence is *modal*. Sometimes if you hadn't had a particular experience, you wouldn't have a particular belief. Causal and modal links between experience and warrant are what we will focus on, but the basic idea is the same. Both of these obvious ideas work well for *a posteriori* warrant – you have the experience of seeing a brown chair in front of you, and this experience earns you some warrant for that belief. The experience caused the belief, and generated its warrant. And if you hadn't had the experience, but retained the belief, the belief would be unwarranted.

There are many wrinkles about causal and modal conditions like this, and their combination, but the overall idea is fairly clear.

The trouble is that it is not obvious that *any* warrant-generating processes are causally or modally independent of experience. We can illustrate this with an

---

[17] My approach is somewhat related to what used to be called "sense-data" theories; see Russell (1912). But the troublesome baggage associated with those theories has been left at home.

example. Mathematics is something like a paradigm domain of the *a priori*. I am *a priori* warranted in believing that there are infinitely many prime numbers. Yet having this belief required learning the ingredient concepts, such as "prime number." This was done – how else? – by way of various experiences, sitting in classrooms, reading books, and so on. Additionally, my belief and its warrant depend on my having worked through Euclid's famous proof of the infinitude of primes in *The Elements*. Experiences caused my belief, and if I hadn't had the experience of working through the proof, I wouldn't have any *a priori* warrant for my belief. These points show that even supposedly paradigm cases of *a priori* warrant causally and modally depend on experience. There are ways to tinker with the conditions to try and avoid this result, but I think it's worth looking for an alternative approach.

Related difficulties are usually brushed aside by explicitly exempting the experiences required to gain the concepts involved in a belief or, equivalently, to learn the meanings of ingredient words. This makes sense. We are interested in the *epistemic* relation of experience to beliefs, and having concepts (or grasping meanings) is a precondition for any having any beliefs at all. But this standard exemption is not enough, for I understood the claim that there are infinitely many prime numbers before I worked through Euclid's proof.[18] In fact, I needed to understand the ingredient notions in order to understand the proof.

To rectify things we need to consider a different condition, one that heeds some of the points about experience noted earlier. Consider again the two paradigmatic examples I've used, one of *a posteriori* warrant and one of *a priori* warrant. In the first, I have an experience of seeing a brown chair in front of me, so I am warranted in believing that there is a brown chair in front of me, *a posteriori*. In the second, I have an experience of working through Euclid's proof of the infinitude of primes, so I am warranted in believing that there are infinitely many primes, *a priori*. In the *a posteriori* case, the theoretical idea that sensory features are caused by the independent external world is crucial. From the inside, this makes nonvoluntariness essential. Yet when experiences are used in generating *a priori* warrant, it is not essential that they were generated by an independent external world. Nor is it relevant that they are generated involuntarily. In fact, if the very same qualitative features of a sensory run were generated in imagination, voluntarily, my warrant would be *exactly the same*.

This is crucial, so let's go over it more carefully. Given that I have all of the ingredient concepts, if I had perfectly imagined Euclid's proof of the infinitude

---

[18] To my knowledge, the only philosopher who has denied this is the later Wittgenstein (1956).

of primes, the infinitude of primes would still have been proven. A proof token in the head is just as good as a proof token in the world. It does not matter. My *a priori* warrant does not depend upon the qualitative features of a sensory run counting as experiential. Take care here to distinguish between (*a*) imagining *that there is a proof* and (*b*) imagining *a proof*. What matters here is only (*b*), the perfect creation of a proof token in the imagination. Merely imagining an announcement that there is a proof, or that all mathematicians believe that there is a proof, is not what we're after.

With this point in hand, we can see the sense in which *a priori* warrant is independent of experience. Suppose some warrant causally or modally depends on an experience. Sometimes when this happens, swapping out the experience for an imaginative act with the *exact same qualitative features* preserves the warrant. In these cases, experience was irrelevant to the warrant. In other words, the warrant is independent of whether the sensory run was actually an experience. Suppose that an experience generates a warranted belief; then:

> The warrant is *a priori* just in case if the belief generated by the experience had instead been generated in the same way by a non-experiential sensory run qualitatively identical to the experience, the belief would have had the exact same content and overall epistemic status.[19]

This is put in terms of the settled concept of an experience. In terms of the *prima facie* concept, the point is that voluntarily produced perfect qualitative simulations of a sensory run are sometimes just as good, as evidence (so to speak), as actual experiences. When an experience passes this <u>imagination test</u> we say that the experience played only an <u>enabling</u> role in warranting the belief in question. I think this also covers the experiences required to learn concepts and meanings, but if not, we can explicitly stipulate that they are enabling – likewise for broad, mediating background conditions. When an experience plays a non-enabling, epistemically relevant role, then we say it plays an <u>epistemic</u> role.[20]

In short: with *a priori* warrant for beliefs, the fact that something is an experience itself *plays no role in generating the warrant*. An imaginative recreation of the experience would have been just as good, epistemically speaking, provided it fits into the same structural chain of reasoning. It would have generated the exact same warrant, in either case. This condition is obviously not satisfied by *a posteriori* warrant. An experience of a brown chair in front of me warrants my belief that there is a brown chair in front of me, but

---

[19] The "content" clause is to ensure that we are still considering the exact same claim in the cases we are comparing and that we retain all of the ingredient concepts or meanings.

[20] The enabling role is related to Chalmers's (2012) causal and mediating (as opposed to justifying) roles that experience can play in belief generation.

merely imagining a brown chair in front of me does not. This is an absolutely fundamental difference.

You might worry about how this condition handles cases where you learn something about yourself from experience. Indeed, the imagination test arguably overgenerates if we consider beliefs about our capacities that are witnessed by qualitative sensory runs – my belief that I am capable of seeing blue probably should not count as *a priori*, at least in the sense relevant for defining *a priori* truth. Let us exclude these qualitative witnessing cases by stipulation. Other cases of self-knowledge are well-handled. I see red and become enraged. Based on this experience, I form the belief that red pisses me off. Imagining this does not lead to the same warrant, since it requires imagining the whole experience, including the anger. This is the same reason you don't learn much about yourself directly from dreams (absent a Freud-style theory of the unconscious mind).

Overall, this way of drawing the enabling versus epistemic distinction neatly isolates the key role of experience in *a posteriori* warrant and its absence in *a priori* warrant. It explains why you could, in principle at least, have *a priori* warrant from not only the armchair, but also from the inside of a sensory deprivation chamber, or even as a brain in a vat. This is exactly what we expected and wanted from a characterization of *a priori* warrant. Further refinements and details could be added, and objections and challenges considered, but I think enough has already been said to broadly convey the overall idea. This idea is important in getting us close to the heart of the *a priori*, but the most important overall point is that we all need to somehow isolate merely enabling experiences in order to maintain a standard conception of *a priority*.

We can now distinguish between the two different kinds of *a priori* warrant – *a priori* entitlement and *a priori* justification. Recall that entitlement is the externalist type of warrant, justification the internalist type. Someone could accept one of these types of *a priori* warrant but not the other. And nothing in this setup begs the question in favor of either externalism or internalism in epistemology.[21]

This explains the key kind of "independence" required for *a priori* warrant in terms of forming beliefs. But there is another natural thing that is sometimes meant by saying that warrant is "independent" of experience – that the warrant cannot be defeated or undermined by experience. If this kind of warrant exists, it is completely immune to empirical defeat. If you have this kind of warrant, and you have some further experiences, you still have the *a priori* warrant you

---

[21] In particular, the characterization of enabling roles does *not* implicitly assume that warrant derives only from the qualitative features of a relevant internal state.

started with, provided you retain all of the relevant concepts throughout the process.[22] Call this robust *a priori* warrant. It is part of what many philosophers have in mind in their discussions of the *a priori*.[23]

There are some obvious objections to the very existence of robust *a priority*. For one thing, it seems that any warrant whatsoever can be undermined in a social fashion. Suppose you learn that all of the world's mathematicians now agree that numbers over a million do not exist. This information seems to undermine your warrant for believing that there are infinitely many prime numbers. On the basis of the information, you might even suppose that there must be an extremely subtle flaw in Euclid's proof that previously escaped your notice. If experience can lead us to *rationally* reject any claim, then robust *a priority* is undermined. Using points like this, some philosophers have argued that no warrant is robustly *a priori*.[24]

This argument is not completely watertight. For one thing, it doesn't seem like your warrant is undermined or added to by social factors if it is considered in a suitably idealized sense. In idealizing we set aside computational errors of all kinds. So once we idealize in this way, we eliminate the possibility of an unnoticed flaw in the proof.[25] It also isn't clear that social factors can undermine *a priori* entitlement even if they can undermine *a priori* justification. In any case, let me simply stipulate that what is at issue with robust *a priority* is direct undermining. This is undermining or defeat that does not go by way of anyone else's beliefs or thoughts about the matter at issue. Say that warrant is robustly *a priori* just in case it cannot be defeated directly by experience.

Let's combine all of these points into the following simple terminology:

> A claim is weakly *a priori* if it can be warranted *a priori*, but is not robustly *a priori*.

> A claim is strongly *a priori* if it can be robustly warranted *a priori*.

Something like this distinction and terminology is already in the literature.[26] If we show only that some *a priori* warrant exists, we will not yet have shown that robust *a priori* warrant exists, so we won't have shown that any claim is strongly *a priori*. To investigate *a priori* warrant fully we need to consider whether there is any *a priori* entitlement, any *a priori* justification, and finally, whether any *a priori* warrant is robust.

---

[22] This means roughly that there are no empirical *undercutting* defeaters; see Pollock (1987).
[23] See Field (1996), Hempel (1945), and Kitcher (1984) for some examples. Casullo (2003) pushes back against this.
[24] See Kitcher (1984).   [25] A similar point is noted to the same purpose in Field (2000).
[26] See Field (1996).

To spoil my conclusions, I will argue for all three of these kinds of *a priority*. And I will attempt to argue for these conclusions without appeals to magic. To start with the easiest case, let's consider how innate beliefs and mechanisms generate *a priori* entitlements.

3 *A Priority* through Innateness

Almost everyone should accept *a priori* entitlements. At least, that is what I will argue in this section. My argument concerns the epistemic status of innate beliefs and rules.

Consider the case of Robbie the robot – an artificial intelligence designed by an advanced A. I. laboratory. As a robot, Robbie takes in rich sensory information about the world, behaves in various ways, and even generates speech. He is a cognitive agent in the same way that humans are cognitive agents. This despite the fact that Robbie was designed by tech nerds while the tech nerds themselves were "designed" by Mother Nature. Let's suppose also that Robbie, sophisticated though he is, is highly susceptible to water damage. If Robbie were submerged in water, his system would catastrophically crash.

To best equip Robbie for success, his designers decide to directly hard-code certain beliefs into his intricate cognitive system. One of these being the belief that water is dangerous (to him). In other words, Robbie believes that he will be harmed by water.[27] On the first day of his artificial life, Robbie opens his electronic eyes and faces the cruel world. At that very moment, by hypothesis, Robbie already *believes* that water will harm him. He may not be able to verbalize it yet, and he may not be making an occurrent judgment about it, but in some sense, he is "born" with this belief.

At this initial moment, does Robbie have warrant for believing that water will harm him?

By hypothesis, Robbie lacks evidence for this belief, so let's start by assuming that he doesn't have any justification either. Since he has had no experiences at all, any entitlement he has could not be generated by and does not depend on his experiences. Does he have any entitlement for his water belief? The question concerns the status of innate beliefs, as such. I think that Robbie has an epistemic right to this belief, so he must be entitled to it. If he wasn't entitled, he wouldn't be warranted, so he'd be making some kind of mistake in holding the belief.[28] What mistake could this be? Psychologically, his cognitive system

---

[27] That is, Robbie has a *de se* belief, not merely the belief that Robbie the robot is harmed by water.

[28] I think we can say this without fully embracing a "deontological" conception of justification; see Alston (1988).

is functioning exactly as it was designed to function. So I think we should say both that Robbie has some entitlement for this belief and that he is provisionally entitled to the belief. That is, he not only has entitlement, but his entitlement passes the salient threshold, making his belief epistemically appropriate.

What goes for Robbie's water belief also goes for any other innate belief. I don't know if humans actually have innate beliefs. It is sometimes said that we innately believe that snakes and heights are dangerous. I think this probably overstates things. I doubt that Mother Nature supplies us with concepts of anything but a rudimentary sort, and innate concepts seem required for innate beliefs.[29] I once sat next to a retired high school biology teacher on a long train trip. During the trip, he told me about an experiment he would perform with his students. A "v"-shaped bit of cardboard was set on a clothesline above some chicks at midday. If you pulled the line in one direction, the chicks ignored the cardboard's shadow and went about their merry business. But if you pulled it in the opposite direction, they scattered. The explanation he provided was that only in the latter direction did the cardboard's shadow resemble a hawk.[30] It would be too much to credit chicks with the innate belief that hawks are dangerous, or even that hawk shadows look a certain way. For similar reasons, I'm skeptical that humans have innate beliefs, but *if* we do, we are provisionally entitled to those beliefs *by default*. Likewise, Robbie is entitled to his belief that water is dangerous. This entitlement is trivially independent of experience, so it is *a priori*. Voila.

I suspect that most externalists will agree with this. Though some of them will think that entitlements to innate beliefs exist only when the beliefs are true, or only when they are induced by reliable processes. Whatever extra conditions are imposed, most externalists will allow that believers can sometimes have *a priori* entitlements to innate beliefs. Above I assumed that Robbie's belief was unjustified, but some internalists can take my argument for entitlement to apply to justification just as well. Though justification that requires cognitive access will have to wait.

At the very least, there is a reasonable case for *a priori* entitlement to innate beliefs. This sounds important, but don't get too excited about it. This *a priori* warrant is obviously not robust. Robbie can lose the entitlement to his water belief in various ways. Also, recall from Section 2 that *being innate* is not a belief-forming method, so *a priority* through innateness doesn't help us cordon off the *a priori* truths.

Let's turn from innate beliefs to innate rules or principles of belief formation. Suppose now that Robbie's programmers build into his cognitive system

---

[29] Fodor (1981) infamously argued that most of our concepts are innate.
[30] In fact, this so-called "hawk/goose" effect is well known; see Schleidt *et al.* (2011).

fundamental rules of belief formation, including the method of forming beliefs on the basis of perception along with basic logical rules for deduction, induction, and abduction.

At this initial moment, is Robbie entitled to form beliefs on the basis of (for example) perception?

I'm even more strongly inclined to accept default entitlement here. Robbie could not possibly be doing anything epistemically inappropriate by employing his in-built methods of belief formation and reasoning, at least provisionally. Most externalists will agree, though some of them will again place some additional constraints. For instance, some of them might think Robbie is only entitled to use methods that are sufficiently reliable in circumstances like those he finds himself in. Even still, almost all externalists will grant the potential existence of *a priori* warrant for innate belief-forming methods.

Perhaps a few externalists would push back against this. They might instead adopt a nonstandard picture where Robbie starts without any entitlement, but then as he forms various beliefs on the basis of perception or the like, if more and more of these beliefs are true, he *eventually* and *gradually* gains entitlement for his methods and the beliefs generated and sustained by them. This is a strange idea. It requires thinking that it is only by first doing something that is not epistemically appropriate that Robbie is able to start doing something epistemically appropriate. It also isn't clear why what Robbie *actually does* should matter so much for externalists. Presumably his in-built methods are either reliable in our world or not, and Robbie's idiosyncratic experiences with them don't seem all that important from an externalist perspective. All told, I think externalists will be even more apt to accept *a priori* entitlement to innate belief-forming methods than they were to accept *a priori* entitlement for innate beliefs.

Can hard-line internalists resist this conclusion about warrant for using innate belief-forming methods? I have my doubts. At the very least, internalists who try are in a difficult position here. Suppose they claim that you can only appropriately use a belief-forming method if you have justification for doing so. On one approach, this requires a justified belief that the method is reliable. How is this belief *itself* justified? It too must have been formed using some belief-forming method. So in order for the belief to be justified we must have antecedent justification for believing that *this method* is reliable. If the second method is the same as the first, we are mired in circularity. If it is different, a regress threatens. Either way, it seems impossible for the process of justification to get started. There is a tight circle here. To have a justified belief, it must be formed using a justified belief-forming method. And to have justification for using a belief-forming method, we are presently assuming, you must first have a justified belief that the method is reliable.[31] Something like this trap will catch many different kinds of internalism.

I don't think that hard-line internalist can find a way out of the trap by insisting that the justification for using a method is somehow gained *a posteriori*, from experience. As long as any justification for using a method takes the form of a belief about the method, they face a serious challenge. Of course, many internalists reject this requirement. They might instead argue that Robbie is justified in using innate methods almost trivially. I won't survey their options. The master point is that without default warrant it is difficult to tell a plausible story about mundane epistemic achievements. So there is pressure on us to allow that Robbie is provisionally warranted in using his innate belief-forming methods, *a priori,* and by default. If he is not entitled to them and has no justification, then as far as epistemology is concerned, he ought not to use them. Epistemology then demands that he simply sits like a rock, belief-less and inert, evermore.

The case for innate rules is made even stronger by the reflection that, at some level, innate cognitive rules are impossible to reject. Without some kind of innate mechanisms, belief formation can never get off of the ground. This is probably why everyone in the history of philosophy has accepted innate cognitive mechanisms. Yes, *everyone*. Literally. Even canonical empiricists and opponents of "innate ideas" like Locke and Hume accepted cognitive processes that were not learned from experience – mainly principles of association.[32]

Of course, these innate cognitive mechanisms need not be belief-forming mechanisms. They might instead be simpler mechanisms that eventually, perhaps with a boost from experience, give rise to belief-forming mechanisms. All the same, we will eventually require the epistemic appropriateness of our most fundamental cognitive mechanisms for forming beliefs, in a default, *a priori* sense, if cognition – and cognitive achievement – is even to begin. This gives us our first sense of *a priority*, without magic.

To once again be a killjoy, I remind you that this default *a priority* through innateness is not the interesting kind that most philosophers have been after.[33] There is no reason to think that our warrant for these beliefs and mechanisms is robust and every reason to think it is not. At best, this kind of "default

---

[31] Chapter 1 of Bonjour (1998) argues that *a priori* justification is needed to extend our beliefs beyond the contents of our immediate experiences. Bonjour seems to think that *a priori* justification for principles of extension can be provided on rationalist grounds, thus providing an internalist way out. I am not sure exactly how this is supposed to work if applied to belief-forming rules themselves. A rule-circular approach could be tried, but it is difficult to see how to do so in line with some versions of internalism.

[32] Mares (2011) makes a similar point.

[33] There are some exceptions; see Goldman (1999), for example.

reasonableness" gives us only weak *a priority*.[34] Remember too that if innateness counts as a belief-forming method, then anything goes, so we need to look elsewhere to flesh out an account of *a priori* truths. But before offering my own non-magical theory of strong *a priority*, I will critically consider so-called rationalist approaches aimed at delivering *a priori* justification.

4 Against Rationalism

Some philosophers still shudder at the mere mention of *a priori* justification. This is probably because the traditional theory of *a priori* justification is an extreme form of <u>rationalism</u>.

The traditional rationalists thought that certain truths about reality were accessible using <u>pure reason</u>. Usually this was understood as a faculty of the mind, similar to perceptual faculties, that allowed us direct access to certain truths of reason. Obviously, humans reason, nobody denies this. But the emphasis here is on *pure* reason – reason uncontaminated by input from the senses. There is a certain internal coherence to this idea. If a little bit of something is good, then a lot of it must be better, and it alone, in pure form, is perfection. This is how six-year-olds argue themselves into eating pure sugar. And while the philosophical idea of pure reason doesn't lead to cavities and an upset stomach, other dangers lie in wait.

It isn't mysterious to think the human mind can access mind-*dependent* facts. In fact, it is so non-mysterious that positing a faculty of pure reason to explain it is akin to using a 44 magnum on a mosquito. Traditional rationalists were aiming for something much grander. They believed that pure reason accessed mind-*independent* facts about reality. According to philosophical folklore, the rationalists eventually went too far, with Hegel supposedly "proving" *a priori* that there were and could only be seven planets in our solar system. It makes for a good cautionary tale, but the folklore is wrong. This favorite example of rationalist overreach probably never happened.[35] So it was not as bad *as all that*, but it was bad enough. Canonical rationalists like Descartes, Spinoza, and Leibniz all thought that facts about the existence of God and the nature of the physical universe could be established *a priori*.

Even aside from any overreach, extreme rationalism is untenable. The decisive objection is simple: there is no faculty of pure reason. Our best guide to human cognition comes from the evolving deliverances of contemporary cognitive psychology and neuroscience. The final words in this story have not

---

[34] For the term "default reasonableness" and similar thoughts, see Field (2000).
[35] See Beaumont (1954).

been written, but no credible hypothesis in these areas posits anything remotely like pure reason. Nor are future scientific discoveries likely to change this.

A modern-day extreme rationalist might object: obviously no cognitive system in the brain carries a *label* saying "rational faculty" or "pure reason happening here" or anything like that. Nonetheless, they might continue, if you work backwards from the assumption that the human mind has this kind of capacity, and you assume that the mind results from the operations of the brain, then you must – *must!* – assume that somehow, someway, pure reason results from the global operation of the human brain. In taking this step, they begin to distance themselves both from old-fashioned faculty psychology and also from the mysterious nature of pure reason.[36]

The trouble with this reply is that it deprives the rationalist hypothesis of content. The rationalist has now retreated from any tolerably precise claims about mental faculties or operations. In their place, we have only fuzzy assertions without empirical content. Against any substantive version of extreme rationalism, the scientific criticism remains decisive: given everything we know about the mind and the world, we have no reason for positing anything like a faculty of pure reason. This is no longer controversial.

Yet rationalism continues to tempt philosophers. I think the temptation is mainly owed to a familiar kind of phenomenology. All of us recall thinking about a riddle for a time before suddenly *getting it*. When this happens, it is an almost irresistible metaphor to say that you suddenly "see" the right answer. This is part of what motivates rationalism, in all its forms. But opponents of rationalism are *not* committed to denying the existence of this phenomenology of understanding.

We all should agree that sometimes we suddenly "see" that a claim is true. When this happens, we not only abruptly gain a disposition to accept the claim, we also abruptly gain several other dispositions at the same time – to connect the claim's truth to our background knowledge, to offer explanations of the claim's truth, and so on. The "explanations" we offer in these situations may fall short of being proofs or they may not. Think again of suddenly seeing the answer to a riddle, or of suddenly solving a chess puzzle. Most of the time, though perhaps not always, we expect such insights to be accompanied by an ability to *spell things out*, to explain why the claim is true and to connect the insight to our background beliefs.

Nothing about this requires a faculty of pure reason. This point is accepted by modern-day rationalists as well as their opponents. Belief in the faculty of pure

---

[36] A modern version of something like faculty psychology is championed by Fodor (1983), but Fodor's naturalistic approach eschews anything remotely like a faculty of pure reason.

reason is (thankfully) going the way of the Dodo bird. Extreme rationalism is, if not quite extinct, at least seriously endangered. But a more modest rationalism remains a significant minority view in epistemology.[37] Modest rationalists drop the idea of a faculty, but stick with quasi-perceptual mental states that are supposed to justify certain beliefs *a priori*. Although this word is overused, I'll follow most of them in calling these states "intuitions." The important qualification is that these are *intellectual* intuitions.

This is something like what was supposed to be delivered by the faculty of pure reason, but without the faculty. Some things *seem* to be the case. It seems, upon looking, that the flag is crimson. It seems that the building is over 500 feet tall. These are perceptual seemings. They are intuitions about what is true given certain perceptual inputs. The idea of an intellectual seeming is based on an analogy to perception. The analogy is needed because these seemings are supposed to be entirely intellectual. You have some perception-like state that tracks truths in domains like logic and mathematics.[38] Several contemporary theories have been given, differing over the fine-grained details.[39] Modest rationalist theories agree that these intellectual intuitions are neither beliefs nor even inclinations to believe. They are instead akin to perception-like states that give rise to inclinations to believe.

Are intellectual intuitions experiences? No, at least not in the relevant sense that I specified in Section 2, for they are not caused by the external world. Despite being involuntary, their connection to reality is much more obscure. I'll say more about this later. If intuitions are not experiences then believing something on the basis of an intellectual intuition that it is true provides *a priori* justification for believing it. Any experiences that accompany these intuitions are merely enabling. Contemporary rationalists typically allow that intellectual intuitions, though they can serve as justifiers, are fallible. It is sometimes possible to have an intellectual intuition that something is true despite it being false. They also allow that we can become aware of having an intuition. In other words, intellectual intuitions are accessible to introspection, though how accessible is a matter of disagreement. It might take work or theoretical reflection to introspectively recognize that you are having an intel-lectual intuition. Still: you can reliably but not perfectly determine when you're having one of these intuitions. This move allows modest rationalism to support

---

[37] I would prefer the term "moderate rationalism," but both Bonjour (1998) and Peacocke (2000) use that term for very different theories. Peacocke's theory doesn't count as a version of "rationalism," by my lights.

[38] Rationalists disagree on the range of truths open to *a priori* justification in this fashion. Some, like Bonjour (1998), limit their rationalism to necessary truths.

[39] For examples, see Bealer (2000), Bengson (2015), Boghossian (2020b), Bonjour (1998), and Chudnoff (2013).

a priori justification even on the assumption of very strong forms of internalism that require cognitive access.

To be plausible, intellectual intuitions can't be some faint glow of reason that lights up whenever we contemplate true mathematical claims of any complexity. Instead, the intuitions are present for axioms and basic principles in mathematics and other *a priori* domains, as well as for certain fundamental rules of inference. This allows a rationalist account of our normal ways of extending our beliefs from axioms or basic principles using rules of inference.[40]

Against modest rationalism, I must first report that I recognize nothing like these states in myself. Perhaps I am defective? Perhaps. Yet it is worth noting that Timothy Williamson, no friend of mine on the *a priori* (see Sections 7 and 8), reports similarly of himself.[41] Do *you*, dear reader, have any intellectual intuitions? What is it like to watch them come and go? Can you feel them fade in and fade out? If you can, your inner life is very different from mine. Nor are intuitions attested in the many efforts of novelists and poets to explore our inner lives. Nor are they appealed to in cognitive science. Like its extreme cousin, modest rationalism sits ill with everything that introspection, art, and science teach us about ourselves.

We can do justice to the phenomenology of *gestalt* understanding without positing intellectual intuitions. And since we can, we should, for there is no other empirical or theoretical reason for accepting rational intuitions. I propose that we explain the feeling of understanding by appealing to our accessible inclinations to accept particular claims, *alone*.[42] I say this as a point in psychology, not epistemology. Psychologically there is, as I have already allowed, a fairly distinct phenomenology associated with the sudden onset of inclinations to accept certain claims. These inclinations are constituted by certain dispositions involving the claim. They are themselves dispositional states that are sometimes (imperfectly) accessible to introspection. Yet if you strip away all of these dispositions, *nothing else remains behind*. There is certainly nothing perception-like remaining behind, however weak we make the analogy to perception. It is far better to think that our nearly automatic inclinations to accept certain claims can be delivered by our unconscious psychological faculties in a variety of mundane ways. There is no need for intellectual intuitions.

Consider a theory that drops intellectual intuitions but holds that some of our considered dispositions to believe claims upon understanding them generate *a priori* warrant. This is an appealing approach, but it isn't a version of

---

[40] Bonjour (1998) stresses this.   [41] In Williamson (2020a).
[42] Related points are made in Sosa (1996), Cappelen (2012), and Williamson (2020b).

rationalism, by itself. To vindicate this kind of theory, we need an account of *which* dispositions to believe claims provide *a priori* warrant for believing them, and *why*. We already know that we have many cognitive biases that lead to errors. Some of these errors easily wash away with reflection, but others may not. The next section offers a theory of how and why some of our dispositions to believe claims on understanding them – though not all – provide *a priori* warrant of the strongest kind.

We can explain all that needs explaining, in both cognition and phenomenology, without intellectual intuitions. This puts significant pressure on modest rationalism. The best explanation of what is happening here is that modest rationalists have put an obscure overlay on top of hum-drum inclinations to believe claims upon understanding them. For these reasons, I reject intellectual intuitions and think we should account for the *a priori* without them.

Let me end this section on a more speculative note. Beyond the phenomenology of understanding discussed earlier, I *think* that the appeal of modest rationalism is tied to pervasive hopes for metaphysical realism in noncausal domains like mathematics, morality, and logic. Realist theories see the facts about these subjects as objective and completely independent of our thoughts and practices. Despite the historical popularity of realism in these areas, it is very hard to see how realism is compatible with our access to the facts in these domains. This is because these domains are not causally connected to us. In fact, they can't be causally connected to us, in principle. Given this, it's very hard to understand how we could have non-accidental reliability, entitlement, justification, or knowledge in these subjects, on the assumption of realism.

Intellectual intuitions are tailor-made to allow us access to the objective mathematical, moral, and logical facts. At least, this is a common thought. But the common thought brings confusions. By hypothesis, intellectual intuitions are not causally connected to the facts in these domains. And on the assumption of standard types of metaphysical realism in these areas, *they couldn't be*, since the facts in these domains are causally inert. Then how do intellectual intuitions provide us with justification for our beliefs in these domains? Not only is there no plausible story to tell, it seems impossible *in principle* to tell any plausible story about this.[43] Seen in this light, modest rationalism is an attempt to smuggle causal mechanisms into a party from which causal mechanisms have been barred. In other words: the connection to mind-independent facts offered by rationalists is either a disreputable causal

---

[43] This is related to the famous epistemological challenges from Benacerraf (1973) and the introduction to Field (1989), except the challenge here concerns an internalist notion of justification. See Warren (2017) for relevant discussion of the target of these arguments. See also the discussion in Section 9.

connection mislabeled or completely mysterious. Either way, no comfort for metaphysical realists can be found here.

So I reject both the extreme rationalist's account of the mind's rational faculties as well as the modest rationalist's special mental states. We can do all of the non-magical work done by these posits by instead allowing for imperfectly accessible and differently explained inclinations to believe certain things upon reflecting on them with understanding. A theory of how *some* of these inclinations and related dispositions give rise to *a priori* warrant will now be offered.

5 A Theory of the *A Priori*

Next to rationalism, the most historically popular family of theories of the *a priori* are meaning or concept-based theories. I won't draw a significant distinction between these. Whether we talk of "meanings" or "concepts" is mainly a matter of whether we want to emphasize language or thought. Either way, the shape of the overall theory of the *a priori* is the same.

The central idea of these approaches is simple: certain truths are merely reflections of what we mean – or of which concepts we employ. The truth that bachelors are unmarried is simply a by-product of what we mean by "bachelor" and the other ingredient words. As such, knowing that it is true does not require investigating the world. By contrast, the truth that there are more bachelors today than there were fifty years ago is not merely a by-product of what we mean. Knowing it requires a serious empirical investigation of the world. The basic contrast I'm drawing right now is very close to the old contrast between analytic and synthetic truths, though it will emerge in Section 6 that the meaning-based theory is a broader and more flexible than this might suggest. The reflection metaphor can be fleshed out and made more precise as an explanatory claim. Seen in this way, the central idea is that meanings and concepts are well placed to explain how it is that some of our beliefs can be warranted, or even known, independently of experience.

Let's call this the meaning-based theory of the *a priori*. Meaning-based theories have long been popular, but we can't simply look to the canonical sources and be done. Early meaning-based theories lacked both detail and precision, and many of them collapsed important distinctions. Yet a simple strategy can be discerned from the sources. That a claim was analytic, or true in virtue of meaning, or true by definition, or true by convention, or tautological, was supposed to explain the claim's truth, necessity, and *a priority*. The strategy was presaged by Hume's "relations of ideas" account of necessary truths. Yet neither Hume nor any other early empiricist worked out the details. The crucial metasemantic idea behind modern meaning-based theories was independently invented and developed by (respectively) Carnap, Gentzen, and Wittgenstein in the nineteen thirties, with a heavy background influence from the great mathematicians Hilbert and Poincaré.[44] It was embraced whole-heartedly by the logical positivists in the twentieth century.[45] But the specific epistemological details were usually galloped over quickly by the positivists. In part this was because of their equation of analytic, necessary, and *a priori* truth. If you don't cleanly distinguish epistemic notions from semantic and metaphysical notions, you can't possibly offer a sensible, purely epistemic theory.

While logical positivism has more recently waned in overall popularity (to say the least), the positivist-style approach to logic has remained quite popular. These approaches to logic are usually developed with an eye toward non-epistemic matters, but some philosophers – most notably Paul Boghossian in an important series of papers – made progress on a meaning-based theory of the *a priori* for logic.[46] With the lessons of these previous attempts well learned, we are now in a good position to give a streamlined meaning-based general theory of the *a priori*.

As already hinted at, meaning-based theories of the *a priori* are built on top of metasemantic theories – theories about the nature of meaning. I won't go into great detail about the base metasemantics here, since many different ways of developing it can support basically the same epistemological story.[47] The crucial metasemantic idea is that the meanings of some words are constitutively determined by accepting certain sentences involving the word, or by following certain rules governing inferences to or from sentences involving the word. This is a spelling out of the popular slogan that *meaning is use*. To illustrate: meaning what we mean by "bachelor" requires following the inference rule:

$$(B \ intro) \ \frac{\alpha \ is \ a \ bachelor}{\alpha \ is \ unmarried}$$

Where "α" is a schematic letter for terms, so that following the rule $(B \ intro)$ involves following each instance of the rule for particular terms. Obviously, many local mistakes are possible, but if somebody really didn't follow this rule *in any sense*, then they wouldn't mean what we mean by "bachelor." Following this inference rule is directly or indirectly built into the meaning of "bachelor";

---

[44] See Carnap (1937), Gentzen (1964, 1965), Hilbert (1950), Poincaré (1905), and Wittgenstein (1974). Coffa (1991) traces the historical development of the approach from Kant through Carnap and Wittgenstein.

[45] See Ayer (1946) and Reichenbach (1951) for popular expositions.

[46] See Boghossian (1996, 2000, 2001, 2003). Boghossian later came to think his approach needed supplementation with a form of modest rationalism; see Boghossian (2014, 2020b).

[47] A full inferentialist metasemantics for logic and mathematics is in Warren (2020); see especially chapter 3.

the correctness of the rule is part of what determines what "bachelor" means in English. So there is a sense in which understanding "bachelor" in English *requires* following this rule.

I've been talking in terms of meaning, but the same points can be made about concepts. To have our concept of a bachelor, you must follow the rule (*B intro*). If you don't follow the rule (*B intro*), then you lack our concept of bachelor. I have used a simple example, but the same thing goes for our logical and mathematical concepts. For example, to have our concept of the conditional, you must follow the rule of *modus ponens*. And to have our arithmetical concepts, you must be disposed to accept that zero is a number.

Metasemantic theories of this kind are sometimes called inferentialist or inferential role theories, since in them certain inferences and inference rules are meaning-determining or meaning-constituting. Similar theories that focus on the acceptance of particular sentences, rather than inferences, are sometimes instead called implicit definition theories. There is no substantive philosophical difference between these two approaches since axioms can be understood as inference rules with no premises and the single sentence as its conclusion. Both approaches grow out of theories that attempt to explain the mysterious notion of meaning in terms of language use. This is the crucial metasemantic idea lurking behind all plausible meaning-based theories of the *a priori*; it will also encompass dispositions to apply words to physical objects and other kinds of uses, when we move beyond simple logical and mathematical examples (see the discussion immediately following and Section 6 for more on this).

What is key here is that to *understand* the content of a sentence containing the term "bachelor," you *must*, according to these theories, follow the rule of (*B intro*).[48] So far there is no direct connection to epistemology, but a connection is natural. The following is a plausible, explanatory, epistemic principle:

> MEANING ENTITLEMENT CONNECTION: we are automatically entitled to use the meaning-determining rules of our language in all contexts[49]

In a sense, we can suspend these entitlements *explicitly*, like when we instruct a logic student not to use *modus ponens* in a certain proof. But such suspension is practical and has nothing to do with standard epistemology. The MEC principle or something like it was implicitly assumed by most empiricists and logical positivists.[50] It is usually assumed without argument, but there is a very

---

[48] This is true if you *use* "bachelor" yourself. If you don't, there are other senses in which you can "understand" its meaning.

[49] An analogous "meaning justification principle" is just as plausible on many, but not all, types of epistemic internalism.

[50] It was made explicit in Boghossian (2003).

strong indirect theoretical case for this principle or something like it. In addition, there are couple of compelling direct arguments in its favor.

The first is a variant of an argument given by Boghossian.[51] If you are trying to establish some claim involving the words $A_1, A_2, \ldots, A_n$ then you must be automatically entitled to use the rules and principles that determine the meanings of $A_1, A_2, \ldots, A_n$. This is because the very claim you are making with A_1, $A_2, \ldots, A_n$ requires that these terms have the meanings that are determined by said rules and principles. Otherwise, the sentence's meaning could have changed. Boghossian's original version of this argument used a strong "ought implies can" principle: if you ought to try to establish a claim without using the basic principles that determine what it means, then you must be able to at least attempt to do so. Yet you cannot try to establish a claim without using these basic principles, since you can't even entertain the claim without using them. Therefore, it is not the case that you ought to attempt to do so. But this is too strong. You can use the conditional without using *modus ponens*, like when we explicitly bar the use of *modus ponens* in setting a logic problem for students. For this reason, I think my related, weaker argument is a bit better. Its conclusion is only that there is nothing epistemically inappropriate about using these rules and principles in any context. This is what the MEC enshrines.[52]

The second argument is rooted in a way of looking at languages that dovetails with inferentialist approaches. Choosing which basic rules to follow is, in effect, choosing which language to speak. This is analogous to playing a game. And that kind of choice is not an *epistemic* matter at all. It is instead merely practical. So you have a *vacuous* epistemic right here. In other words, you are epistemically entitled to speak any language you want. From this point of view, the MEC enshrines the central idea that choosing a language is a practical matter.[53] Substantive epistemic achievement takes place only after a language is chosen. We could also have stated the same argument in terms of choosing a conceptual scheme. You are automatically entitled to speak any language or adopt any conceptual scheme you like. Though keep in mind that you might be *epistemically* entitled to speak a language or adopt a conceptual scheme that you are unable to speak or adopt for *practical* reasons. Such is life.

These automatic entitlements are *a priori*. They do not depend on any particular experiences, save only for the experiences required to learn the ingredient meanings or concepts. But as discussed in Section 2, those learning experiences are merely enabling. So these entitlements do not depend on any experiences in an epistemic sense. If you had simply imagined the experiences

---

[51] See Boghossian (2000, 2003).
[52] This is a version of an argument given in chapter 6 of Warren (2020).
[53] This argument is also given in chapter 6 of Warren (2020).

and dreamt up the concepts for yourself, your entitlement to use the rules would not be changed. The meaning entitlement connection leads to *a priori* entitlements to use certain fundamental inference rules. This same approach can easily cover the axioms of mathematics and the fundamental logical rules, as well as rules like (*B intro*) that underpin conceptual truths of all kinds.

These entitlements are robustly *a priori* – they cannot be overturned by experience. Of course, future experiences may cause you to give up some meaning-constituting claim or inference rule, but this is not strictly relevant. We are concerned with *a priori* warrant for believing *particular claims*. A claim is not a sentence, but instead a sentence with a particular meaning (or a proposition). So according to the meaning-based approach, anyone who means what we mean by "bachelor" follows the rule (*B intro*) and is entitled to follow the rule. If they give up the rule, they give up the concept, but this is different from having the very same belief while lacking *a priori* warrant for it. And that is all that robust *a priority* rules out. So the meaning-based theory delivers robust *a priori* warrant, thus it delivers strong *a priority*. Challenges to this will be addressed in Section 7.

The *a priori* warrants so-generated also extend beyond the directly meaning-determining rules. Consider the sentence "every bachelor is unmarried." In our language, the claim made by this sentence is an *a priori* truth. We can come to know it *a priori*, in something like the following manner:

1. Jared is a bachelor (assumption)
2. Jared is unmarried (from 1 by (*B intro*))
3. if Jared is a bachelor, then Jared is unmarried (from 1, 2, discharging 1)
4. every bachelor is unmarried (from 3, universal generalization)

This simple four-line proof has no undischarged premises. The only rules it uses are plausibly meaning-determining rules which, by the MEC, we are entitled to use in any context. This proof is therefore one we are epistemically entitled to. In other words, entitlement is preserved when we use our basic rules to derive sentences – or even non-basic rules.[54] So anything that we can prove using our rules is something we can, in principle, gain an *a priori* entitlement to according to the meaning-based theory of the *a priori*. It might be true that only working through a proof using our basic rules generates this entitlement, but as was discussed in Section 2, the experience of working through the proof is merely enabling. If we had simply imagined the proof, in perfect detail, with every step intact, we would still be entitled to its conclusion.

---

[54] This is related to why we didn't need to say that (*B intro*) is a *directly* meaning-determining rule.

There are different ways to use the meaning-based theory to give an account of *a priori* justification, as opposed to *a priori* entitlement. If justification doesn't demand cognitive access, then the story I have told for entitlement could just as well have been told for justification. For the same reasons then, being automatically justified in using basic rules extends to justification for accepting claims and rules that are derivable from the basic rules. Experiences involved in the extension process pass the imagination test, so they are merely enabling. On the other hand, if justification does require cognitive access, then meaning-based theories can appeal to occurrent states of accessing the under-lying dispositions. We might call these states of "recognition" or "understand-ing." Suitably spelled out, this mimics the modest rationalist approach, but without positing intellectual intuitions. Other approaches to access-involving justification are possible for meaning-based theorists, some involve imagination in a direct way (see the discussion in 6.6). In any case, both externalist and internalist types of *a priori* warrant are secured by the meaning-based theory. And for meaning-based theories, the step from this to *a priori* knowledge is quite short.

The metasemantics behind meaning-based theories ensures that the meaning-determining rules of our language are *valid* in our language – truth-preserving in the strongest sense. This ensures that the sentences provable using only such rules will be true and necessary in the strongest sense. And this, in turn, ensures that whatever anti-accident condition (Section 1) is required for a belief to count as "knowledge" can be met by meaning-based theories. To mention two popular conditions: the method of proving something using the rules of our language and believing it on that basis generates beliefs that are both *sensitive* to the relevant facts and are also *safe*, in that they couldn't easily have been wrong.[55] The meaning-based theory can be combined with any reasonable philosophical theory of knowledge to explain how conceptual, logical, and mathematical truths are knowable *a priori*.

The meaning-based theory can account for both kinds of *a priori* warrant and *a priori* knowledge, but so far I have covered all and only the canonical, *a priori* necessary truths.[56] In Section 6 I will show that the meaning-based theory of the *a priori* can also account for contingent and synthetic *a priori* warrant as well. Before getting to that, here is a quick Q&A meant to highlight, roughly and quickly, some of the ways in which the meaning-based theory of the *a priori* can be fleshed out.

---

[55] See Nozick (1981) for sensitivity and Williamson (2000) for safety.
[56] There is a worry that not all of these truths are so covered, stemming from arithmetical incompleteness, but even these can be handled; see chapters 10 and 11 of Warren (2020).

Which rules and principles are meaning-determining?

When we are setting up a formal language we can stipulate which rules and principles are meaning-determining. But which natural language inference rules and principles are meaning-determining? Different inferentialists and implicit definition theorists have offered different answers to this question. The most popular answers have a common shape: certain rules are *primitive* or *basic* in a behavioral, psychological sense. They aren't followed because other rules are followed or by way of following more fundamental rules; they are instead followed *directly*.[57] These are the primitive moves in our language game. Obviously, this idea could be spelled out further, but it is extremely difficult to deny that something like this distinction is operative in natural languages. A mathematical axiom like "zero is a number" has a very different status than does a complex mathematical claim like "there is no decision procedure for Diophantine equations." Likewise for simple logical rules like *modus ponens* versus complex but valid rules with thirty premises.

To clarify: my claim here is *not* that any innate rule is meaning-constituting. As I discussed in Section 3, I think we have *a priori* entitlements to follow innate rules. But these are not the kind of automatic *a priori* entitlements being considered here. The *a priority* generated by innateness was instead highly contextual and non-robust. Because of this, innate entitlements as such can be overturned by experience. So to say that a rule is "basic" in the sense required for meaning-determination is not to say that it is innate.[58]

Are there any constraints on which rules can determine meanings?

The standard objection to meaning-based theories is not to the epistemology, but instead to the metasemantics the epistemology is built on. Consider the supposedly meaning-determining inference rules for Prior's "tonk" connective:

$$(tonk\ intro)\ \frac{\phi}{\phi\ tonk\ \psi}\quad (tonk\ elim)\ \frac{\phi\ tonk\ \psi}{\psi}$$

The newly defined connective "tonk" combines the introduction rule for "or" with one of the elimination rules for "and," yet if we assume that these rules are automatically valid for the "tonk" connective, disaster results. From any sentence, we can prove any other sentence. So from the truth "Hume is the greatest Scottish philosopher" we can prove "2 + 2 = 5." What is worse, if there is

---

[57] For examples, see Peacocke (1992) on "primitively compelling inferences," Harman (1986) on "immediate implication," and Schiffer (2003) on "underived conceptual roles." My own account, in terms of "basic" versus "derivative" inference rules, is given in chapter 3 of Warren (2020).

[58] See chapters 2 and 3 of Warren (2020).

a single theorem in our language, then every sentence is a theorem. So we can prove "2 + 2 = 5" from no premises. This seems to be a catastrophe. Nearly everyone has taken tonk to show that the unrestricted inferentialism of Carnap and Wittgenstein needs to be restricted.

Inferentialists have jumped to this task, arguing for this or that restriction on which rules can found meanings or on which meanings are appropriate for the MEC to apply.[59] I think these two restrictions basically come to the same thing, but neither is ultimately required. If language users really and truly follow the tonk rules, they will trivialize their language. A tonk language cannot express any empirical information at all.[60] What is that to us? Tonk languages are silly languages. This is a practical condemnation, not a comment on the nature of meaning or concepts. Yes, our metasemantics might force us to say that "2+2=5" is true in Tonklish, but that does not show that "2+2=5" is true *in English*. To suppose otherwise is to commit what I have elsewhere called the translation mistake. This involves inappropriately adopting a homophonic translation between languages. I think that there is no more fundamental, important, and often-made mistake in philosophy. Claims or statements must be distinguished from the sentences used to make them. I have already elaborated on these points in several other places, so I won't go into detail here.[61]

The central epistemological point is that even in the face of tonk, unrestricted inferentialists can happily opt for a simple and streamlined theory that accepts the full MEC without any incoherence or overgeneration. Restricted inferentialists, by contrast, are forced to restrict the MEC, either explicitly to special concepts or implicitly to those collections of rules that can generate concepts. This complicates the picture considerably, but might not completely break it.[62] In any case, I personally think the unrestricted inferentialist approach is simpler, better, clearer, and more epistemologically plausible.[63]

Does this lead to radical pluralism?

Yes, unrestricted inferentialism leads to radical pluralism. Any collections of rules can found meanings, provided the rules are ones that can be

---

[59] Starting with Belnap (1962).
[60] Unfortunately, Carnap encouraged misunderstanding about this with his purely formal treatment of factual and natural law claims; see sections 5.I, 5.II, 12.V, and 13.II of my 2020 for details and correction. See also Ayer (1940) on "the errors of formalism" (not cited in my 2020 only because I hadn't read it at the time of writing).
[61] See Warren (2015b, 2020).
[62] There are worries about how restricted inferentialists can guarantee *a priori* knowledge, given that our rules can fail to be truth preserving. But though serious, these worries aren't obviously unanswerable.
[63] See chapters 3 and 4 of Warren (2020).

followed in a practice. We can envision alternative logical rules, alternative mathematical rules, and the like. Obviously, everyone already admits that a word like "bachelor" could have been used differently. In some alternative versions of English, "bachelor" could even be used in the way that "dog" is used in actual English. The pluralism I am committed to goes far beyond this platitude.

The controversial pluralism requires that in a language in which the basic rules governing "or" and "not" are not our classical logical rules, but instead the rules of intuitionistic logic, the speakers of said language are using intuitionistic logic. Their words "or" and "not" have their intuitionistic meanings, and the logical truths in that language are the logical truths of intuitionistic logic, not of classical logic. Instead of disagreeing with us, speakers of alternative languages end up talking past us. The idea of different languages with alien rules truly disagreeing with us about analytic truths is a mirage. The mirage vanishes once we stop making the translation mistake.[64]

Aren't some languages or concepts epistemically broken?

No; languages and concepts can be stupid and silly and worthless, but they can't be epistemically inappropriate. Languages are tools. They are the most powerful and flexible tools we have, but tools all the same. When we judge languages or concepts, we judge in practical but not epistemic terms.[65] Let me briefly pump your intuitions for this using a less controversial example. In the twentieth century, Pluto was counted as a "planet"; but early in the twenty-first century, we intentionally altered our usage of "planet" to exclude Pluto and other so-called dwarf planets. Most of us agree that there are decent practical reasons for this linguistic change. On this basis, do you think that English speakers in 1950 were making an *epistemic* mistake in counting Pluto as a "planet"?

I don't. In fact, I think it's absurd to think they were making an epistemic mistake, even an understandable, forgivable epistemic mistake. They were *correctly* using "planet" according to their meaning-determining rules. Suppose someone today persisted in calling Pluto a "planet." While this deviant soul might depart from English as a public language, there is no plausible case that they are making an epistemic mistake in doing so. They are instead expressing claims correctly *in their language*. If we think they are wrong, it is in making a poor practical choice. We disagree with them in our choice of language, not in our beliefs.

---

[64] Conceptual pluralism is fleshed out in Warren (2015a, chapter 5 of 2020).
[65] This is a central theme of Carnap (1950).

Humans gain concepts in various ways. Many of our concepts first came by generalizing from experience. This is true even of various mathematical concepts. But it is an error to argue that this would make mathematics *a posteriori*.[66] The error is akin to a use/mention confusion. In any case, the experiences required to gain concepts have already been factored out (Section 2). We might have instead gained our concepts after being hit on the head with a shovel. Or by taking a pill. It wouldn't matter. However a concept is learned or gained, there may well be truths that come along as by-products of having the concept. Gaining concepts is one thing, applying them is another. Clarity is best served if we take great care not to confuse the epistemic with the merely practical, nor the merely genealogical.

Does this lead to truth by convention and isn't that a problem?

Unrestricted inferentialism does lead to a form of conventionalism.[67] The analytic truths are "true by convention" – they are forced to be true as a trivial by-product of what we mean by those sentences. There are many arguments against conventionalism, but all of them can be answered. I have already told the conventionalist story at great length in *Shadows of Syntax*, at least for logic and mathematics, so I won't retell the full story here. In short: I accept a modern-day conventionalist account of these areas, and I think there is no better theory. My name is "Jared," and I'm a conventionalist. You should be one too (said the unbiased conventionalist).

Many restricted inferentialists think they can accept something like the *a priori* epistemology I have offered here but without any commitment to a metaphysical notion of analyticity, that is, without accepting conventional truths.[68] I have some doubts, but it's a common enough view. Even if it's true, it doesn't undermine my conclusions or the basic theory of the *a priori* I am offering. Restricted inferentialists will just tell a more convoluted version of the same story. Even on these views, where there is *a priori* warrant, it will come in the good cases where it is almost automatic. So the restricted inferentialist will treat those special cases the way that I treat *all* cases.

Doesn't this make *a priori* warrant too easy?

There is a standard objection to meaning-based accounts of the *a priori* – they threaten to make *a priori* warrant too easy to obtain. Fortunately, the objection is deeply confused. Let's illustrate the objection with an example. Goldbach's conjecture is a famous unsolved mathematical problem. It holds that every even

---

[66] Contrast this with the "Aristotelian" positions of Mares (2011) and Jenkins (2008).
[67] Chapter 4 of Warren (2020).   [68] This idea derives from Boghossian (1996).

number greater than two is the sum of two (possibly repeated) prime numbers. The conjecture was first made in the eighteenth century, but to this day it has been neither proven nor refuted. If what I'm saying is right, then we could simply alter our arithmetical language by adding Goldbach's conjecture as a new axiom. If we treated this new axiom as meaning-constituting, then we would have easy *a priori* entitlement for believing the conjecture, which would easily give way to *a priori* justification and knowledge too, in the ways discussed earlier.

The confusion is – yet again – a version of the translation mistake. Goldbach's conjecture is posed in our current language. We can add the Goldbach *sentence* as a new axiom, but that is not the same thing as adding the Goldbach *claim*. If we add new meaning-constituting rules for our language, we alter our practice in a way that changes the meanings of our words in a fine-grained sense, and may even change the meanings of our words and the truth values of our sentences in a coarse-grained sense. All we get from this alternative language is that there is *a priori* warrant for accepting the sentence expressing our Goldbach conjecture *in that alternative practice*. This does not solve Goldbach's conjecture. For that we would need to be able to move from the sentence's truth in that alternative language to the same (syntactically individuated) sentence's truth *in our language*. All paths to that result require solving Goldbach's conjecture by either proving or refuting it in our starting language.

Does the meaning-based theory extend beyond the analytic or conceptual truths?

Most historical proponents of the meaning-based theory have limited their claims to analytic and conceptual truths. Because of this, there haven't been many discussions from meaning-based theorists about how to handle the apparent problem cases outside of logic and mathematics. I rectify this in the next section by briefly considering all of the major challenge cases.

6 Challenge Cases

We have a strong pre-theoretical sense about which truths are accessible *a priori* and which are not. The meaning-based theory might reasonably lead us to reclassify a few cases, but only on the margins. If the theory didn't closely align with our intuitive classifications, it would fail as a descriptive account of the *a priori*/*a posteriori* distinction. Fortunately, the meaning-based theory gives us everything we reasonably may hope for from a theory of the *a priori*, and nothing more. Or so I will argue, through brief discussions of the main challenge cases.

6.1 Memory and Long Proofs

I gave a simple proof in the previous section. That proof was short enough to be taken in "at a glance," in one *gestalt* moment of comprehension. Some proofs are much, much longer. Many contemporary mathematical proofs are dozens or even hundreds of pages long. No human can take in every step in these proofs at a glance. Yet our warrant for believing the conclusions of these proofs is *a priori*. Can we make sense of this?

Rodrick Chisholm argued that we cannot – belief on the basis of long mathematical proofs essentially relies on memory and so is not *a priori*.[69] There is a standard response to this, from Tyler Burge.[70] Burge replied that the role of memory in long proofs was not substantive, but was instead merely preservative. We might try to spell this out with the imagination test (section 2), but any adequate epistemology must recognize at least two different roles that memory can play in cognitive achievement. In simple terms, the key difference is between some reasoning (*a*) relying on memory and (*b*) including claims about memory. If you to ask me what warranted step 57 in a 101-step mathematical proof, I might reply that step 56 justified step 57. Or I might reply by restating the claim made at step 56. What I would *not* do is cite the fact that I remember reaching a particular claim at step 56. I wouldn't because it's not relevant to the question asked. When I move through the 101-step proof, I may rely on my memory at various points, but I do not reason using claims about my memory.

Meaning-based theories of the *a priori* can accept all of these points. What is more: *a priori* entitlement to a long proof comes through *a priori* entitlement to all of the rules and principles used in the proof, nothing else. According to the MEC, these entitlements are automatic for our meaning-determining rules and principles. So clearly memory plays no role in generating the entitlement. To preserve *a priori* justification on the basis of long proofs, meaning-based theorists can adapt Burge's response to Chisholm, though the exact details will depend on the specific account of justification endorsed.[71]

6.2 Testimony

Burge thought his response to Chisholm led to extending the traditional scope of the *a priori*. He argued that we sometimes have a default entitlement to testimonial information. He did not base this on an empirical claim about the

---

[69] In Chisholm (1977).   [70] See Burge (1993).

[71] For proofs that are too long for humans to take in at all, like the classification of finite simple groups, *a priori* entitlement for believing the proof's conclusion is no problem. And there are options for either allowing or disallowing justification in this kind of situation.

reliability of testimony, that would have made the entitlement *a posteriori*. He instead argued that you have a general entitlement to anything presented to you as true that is intelligible to you. He then used this "presentation principle" to secure default, *a priori* entitlement to the deliverances of testimony.[72]

Even if Burge's claims were correct, they would only secure weak *a priority* through testimony. In any case, his claims are not correct.[73] Burge's presentation principle is suspect. In fact, Burge seems to be sliding over something close to the very distinction he himself used against Chisholm. There is a difference between some reasoning (*a*) relying on testimony and (*b*) including a claim about testimony. We need to distinguish between someone telling me *why p* is true, and someone telling me *that p* is true. Only the former is preservative, in the way that the use of memory in a long proof is. In the first case, if I am asked why I believe that *p* I will cite its basis without mentioning the testimony. In the second case, I will cite only the fact that I received the testimony. In the first case, the role of testimony is analogous to the preservative role of memory in long proofs; in the second case, the role of testimony is substantive and explicit, and warrant on this basis is not *a priori* – merely imagining the testimony would not generate the same warrant.

6.3 The Necessary *A Posteriori*

Many historical proponents of meaning-based theories of the *a priori* equated necessity with *a priority*, extensionally speaking. Kripke refuted this simple equation with compelling examples of both necessary *a posteriori* and contingent *a priori* truth.[74] It's natural to wonder how meaning-based theories treat these cases, especially since they were entirely unknown during the heyday of logical positivism.

True identity claims serve as the canonical examples of necessary *a posteriori* truths. Included among these canonical examples are theoretical identity claims like "water is H_2O." This is a necessary truth, it couldn't have been otherwise. Why? Because both the kind term "water" and the molecular description "H_2O" are *rigid* – when they refer, they refer to the same thing in every possible world. Yet rigidity is not a brute fact, but is instead a by-product of how we use language. The full metasemantic story is involved, but at bottom, either directly or indirectly, we follow this inference rule when using "water":

$$(\text{Water}) \quad \frac{\text{water is the same as } F}{\text{water is necessarily the same as } F}$$

---

[72] The presentation principles is a bit like the principle mentioned and rejected in Section 4, where *all* inclinations to believe upon understanding generate actual justification.

[73] For a detailed rebuttal, see Malmgren (2006, 2013).   [74] In Kripke (1980).

Given this it follows that the conditional "if water is the same as H_2O, then water is necessarily the same as H_2O" is an analytic or conceptual *a priori* truth. This isn't in tension with Kripke's arguments though, since the antecedent of this conditional is neither analytic nor *a priori*, and neither is its consequent.

Necessary *a posteriori* truths factor into two distinct components: (1) a factual claim ("water is the same as H_2O") and (2) an analytic linking conditional with said factual claim as its antecedent ("if water is the same as H_2O, then water is necessarily the same as H_2O"). The consequent of this conditional is not accessible *a priori*. Its truth is explained partly in terms of the facts, with (1), and partly in terms of our meaning-determining rules, with (2). Our knowledge of these truths comes by way of gaining empirical information and discharging the conditional. This is what differentiates necessary *a posteriori* truths from necessary *a priori* truths. Using this idea, suitably elaborated, meaning-based theories can naturally and plausibly account for these truths and their *a posteriori* status. I have recently provided this elaboration elsewhere, so I won't say more here.[75]

6.4 The Contingent *A Priori*

The other side of Kripke's coin is the contingent *a priori*. An especially compelling example is Kaplan's sentence, "I am here now."[76] This sentence always expresses a claim that is contingent, but it can be known *a priori* because every utterance of the sentence expresses a truth.

This is grist for the meaning-based mill. Our linguistic rules for using indexical terms like "I" and "now" explain why every utterance of Kaplan's sentence expresses a truth. Warrant for believing its content on any occasion plausibly comes from the basic linguistic rules governing indexical expressions. If all examples of the contingent *a priori* depend on indexicality or something similar, then the category poses no problem at all for meaning-based theories.

All of the now traditional examples of the contingent *a priori* fit into this box.[77] But recently, examples of supposedly non-indexical, supposedly contingent, supposedly *a priori* truths have been offered, including:

(i) There is at least one believer (understood tenselessly)[78]

(ii) Given such-and-such qualitative experiences, the external world exists (because we can infer the consequent, using nondeductive reasoning, on supposition of the antecedent).[79]

(iii) The most unlikely event possible is not happening right now.[80]

---

[75] See Warren (forthcoming); see also Sidelle (1989).   [76] From Kaplan (1989).
[77] See Evans (1979).   [78] From Williamson (1986).
[79] This is based on an example from Hawthorne (2002).   [80] From Turri (2011).

Space constraints preclude detailed discussion of any of these examples.

Briefly though: warrant for believing (i) is not *a priori* unless some kind of hidden indexicality is posited. And when hidden indexicality is posited, (i) falls in line with the standard indexical examples of the contingent *a priori*.

For (ii), the reasoning to this conditional is problematic. In particular, the reasoning uses conditional proof or the like after a nondeductive inference is made from a supposition, something that we should, at the very least, be cautious about.[81] Even aside from this logical point, belief in (ii) is only warranted *a priori* if the nondeductive reasoning principles connecting the supposition and the conclusion themselves are *a priori* (this will be discussed in 6.5).

Finally, with (iii) the guise "most unlikely event possible" is doing all of the work, just as "I" and "here" and "now" did in Kaplan's sentence, and various reference-fixing descriptions did in Kripke's original examples ("the meter rod is one meter long"). If our rules for understanding sentences using this guise generate warrant for accepting them, in some contexts, that is no problem at all for meaning-based theories. It is worth exercising caution though, for as lottery and preface paradoxes show, the connection between outright belief and a high credence is vexed when extreme probabilities are known; (iii) attempts to leverage this vexation in a way we might reasonably resist.

Further examples need to be considered on a case-by-case basis. For now, it suffices to say that meaning-based theories of the *a priori* are compatible with several strategies for accommodating or undermining candidates for contingent *a priori* truth.

6.5 Inductive Reasoning

So far, I have appealed only to standard deductive inference rules in fleshing out my meaning-based theory of the *a priori*. Deductive rules can be logical rules, like *modus ponens*. Or they can be non-logical rules, like (*B intro*) and (*Water*). Deductive rules are of direct relevance to understanding the *a priori*, since they delimit logical or conceptual space – there is no conceptual possibility containing a married bachelor. This talk of "conceptual space" sounds a bit mysterious, but for meaning-theorists it is explained in terms of our overall package of rules for operating with symbols. Validity itself is a reflection of the deductive rules that we employ in our reasoning.

Yet, as we all know, most of our reasoning is not deductive. In philosophy, science, and everyday life we frequently reason in deductively invalid ways. Of

---

[81] See Weatherson (2012).

course, not all invalid reasoning is on a par. The premises of some invalid arguments none-the-less *support* their conclusions in a weaker fashion. Call these invalid but conclusion-supporting arguments inductively strong. In analogy with deductive logic, inductive logic explicitly codifies the rules that make for inductively strong arguments. This immediately raises a number of questions. What is the epistemic status of the rules of inductive logic? Are we robustly *a priori* warranted in using basic inductive rules? That is: can experience defeat our *a priori* warrant for using basic inductive rules? As Section 3 discussed, even if these rules are innate and weakly *a priori* because of it, they need not be *a priori* in a strong sense.

You might think it's easy to describe a situation in which experience defeats our warrant for using basic inductive rules. You might, but you'd be wrong. It isn't *easy* to describe such cases, even if they exist.

Before you object to this, remember that we are not considering high-level beliefs formed using induction, like the belief that all lawyers are liars. Nor are we considering extremely specific inductive rules, like the rule allowing an increase in your confidence that someone is dishonest upon learning that they're a journalist. Instead we are considering only *basic* inductive rules, that is, our fundamental rules for learning from experience. These rules are extremely general, highly abstract, and involve mechanisms of self-correction. Given these points, it's plausible that basic inductive rules are robustly, and hence strongly, *a priori*.[82]

The meaning-based theory of the *a priori* can account for this by appealing to a controversial but – in my view – defensible idea. The idea I have in mind is sometimes called "logical" or "inductive" probability. Inchoate versions of it were sketched by Bolzano and Wittgenstein, but it was first developed in detail by John Maynard Keynes.[83] The approach flowered in the work of Carnap and his followers in the mid-twentieth century.[84] The central philosophical claim behind logical probability is that there are *logical* relations of *partial* entailment between sentences, with full entailment (deductive validity) as a limiting case.

As a simple illustration, consider natural language disjunctive expressions. The expression "member of Congress" applies just in case "Senator or Representative" applies. And the expression "big cat" applies just in case "lion or tiger or jaguar or leopard or snow leopard or cheetah or cougar" applies. Now consider the following rule of inference:

$$(Lion) \quad \frac{a \text{ is a big cat}}{a \text{ is a lion}}$$

---

[82] Field (2000) argues for this at some length.　　[83] In Keynes (1921).
[84] Most of this work is technical, but much of Carnap (1962) is accessible.

This rule is *not* valid. Despite this, our language, our conceptual scheme, has set up *some* connection between the premise and the conclusion. We have seen that deductively valid rules structure conceptual space in a direct manner; the paths from their premises to their conclusion are inexorable in conceptual space. What I am stressing is that conceptual space has more structure than just this, as the "big cat" example illustrates. The paths from the premise of (*Lion*) to its conclusion are *exorable* in conceptual space, but extant. There are also symmetrical paths from "big cat" to six other feline terms. Rationally speaking, the information that something is a big cat is, *by itself*, neutral between it being a lion, tiger, jaguar, leopard, snow leopard, cheetah, or cougar. Empirical information about the population sizes cannot be built into the language itself. Yet the basic connections *are* part of our linguistic and conceptual framework, and they shape our conceptual space as surely as valid rules do.

The *formal* project of inductive logic is to develop a mathematical theory of partial entailment elaborating this philosophical picture. We could try to do this in a purely qualitative fashion, but it is more common to introduce a numerical measure function to define numerical, conditional probabilities over the entire language. A crucial part of this formal project is recognizing and characterizing the default epistemic state of a believer within a particular linguistic or conceptual framework. In other words, the logical probability approach requires singling out *a priori* prior probabilities. This is usually done by recognizing symmetries in a conceptual space and using them in defining acceptable *a priori* prior probabilities. In fact, I already implicitly did something like this previously when discussing the "big cat" example. This is also what motivates acceptance of the so-called principle of indifference. Perhaps incautious formulations of indifference go too far, but something about babies and bathwater comes to mind.

The logical approach to probability is currently a minority position, but it is a growing one.[85] I not only accept logical probabilities, I am optimistic that they can be understood by, to some extent, assimilating inductive logic to deductive logic, with probabilistic claims in our metalanguage playing a similar role to validity claims in the same. Nobody has yet walked to the end of this particular path, but the early portion of the path is covered with footprints from Bolzano, Keynes, Wittgenstein, Carnap, and other luminaries.

In sum: meaning-based theorists who think that basic inductive rules are robustly *a priori* can accommodate this by endorsing a logical probability approach to inductive logic. Of course, not every meaning-based theorist will

---

[85] For recent endorsements of logical probability or something close to it, see Bradley (forthcoming), Franklin (2001), Huemer (2009), Maher (2006), and Williamson (2010).

agree that our basic inductive rules are robustly *a priori*. Those who do not can safely reject the project of inductive logic, at least as far as the *a priori* is concerned. The crucial dialectical point is that meaning-based theorists have options here.

6.6 The Synthetic *A Priori*

We know many facts about colors. These include color exclusion claims – anything that is red all over is not green. As well as color containment claims – anything crimson is red. Color generalizations like these have often been given as examples of the *a priori*. It seems that anyone who is a master of our color concepts is in position to have warrant for believing them. Despite this, many philosophers doubt that these color generalizations are analytic, probably because unlike "bachelor," color terms don't obviously have neat and tidy explicit definitions.[86]

Put into the terms of Section 5, these philosophers are doubting that this rule is (or follows from) one of our meaning-determining principles for color terms:

$$(C \ to \ R) \ \frac{\alpha \ is \ crimson}{\alpha \ is \ red}$$

Personally, I think that $(C \ to \ R)$ may well be a meaning-determining rule for "crimson" in English. Let's leave that aside though. Even if $(C \ to \ R)$ is a rule of English, it might not have been. We might have instead learned to master the concept of crimson (and red) without learning the $(C \ to \ R)$ rule. This is because enough skill in recognizing objects as crimson (or red) suffices for mastering these color concepts. This point can be made without abandoning the use-based metasemantics sitting underneath the meaning-based theory of the *a priori*. When we look beyond logic and mathematics, our meaning-determining rules and principles of use go beyond standard deductive inference rules that link sentences to a sentence.

Assuming that $(C \ to \ R)$ is not a meaning-determining rule, what should a meaning-based theory say about our belief that all crimson things are red? Can we allow it to be warranted *a priori*? I think so. Suppose that I see a number of samples of crimson and I use my skill in applying the concept of red to judge all of them red. As my sample size grows, my rational confidence that all crimsons things are red grows as well. These experiences don't give me conclusive evidence for the claim, but they do make the claim more likely to be true. I have told this story with an appeal to experiences, but notice that these experiences are merely enabling. If I had only imagined the samples of crimson

---

[86] The inability to handle the color exclusion case is what drove Wittgenstein to abandon the system of the *Tractatus*; see Wittgenstein (1929).

and then applied my concept of red to them *in imagination*, the epistemic status of my conclusion would be exactly the same. So I have some *a priori* warrant for believing that all crimson things are red. My warrant is rooted in my mastery of the concepts of crimson and red.

In this case, we have *a priori* warrant for a true, but non-analytic, necessary claim. Though the claim is not analytic, my *a priori* warrant for believing it is still explained using meaning-determining linguistic rules.[87] It is just explained in a different way. The physical connections of containment between my "crimson" dispositions and my "red" dispositions play a role here.

In saying this, I am cracking the door open for synthetic *a priori* truths. By assumption, the possibility of a crimson thing that is not red is not ruled directly incoherent by our linguistic rules, so we don't rule it out in exactly the same way we rule out married bachelors and round squares. It is still ruled out, just less directly. Under our supposition, there is nothing baldly incoherent about *describing* something as a color experience that counts as an instance of "crimson" without also counting as an instance of "red." The meaning-determining application conditions of "red" wholly contain the meaning-determining application conditions of "crimson," but we can only determine this *indirectly* – by imagining examples, by failing to imagine a counterexample, and so on.[88] This is why (according to our assumption) we don't have just another derived rule, but instead a real example of the synthetic *a priori*.

Yet this doesn't open the door to all supposed examples of the synthetic *a priori*. Meaning-based theorists should only admit cases that can be fully accounted for using our meaning-determining uses of symbols.

6.7 God and Hardcore Metaphysics

Against this, traditional rationalists thought we had *a priori* warrant for believing that God exists, along with many other claims of heavyweight metaphysics. This is impossible to vindicate on meaning-based theories. With apologies to friends of the ontological argument, what we mean by "God" cannot support any of the substantive claims of traditional metaphysics or theology. Introducing some new rule using the word "God" is no help either. You might

---

[87] There is an ambiguity when we apply "analytic" to rules. Sometimes it applies only to basic, meaning-determining rules, at other times it applies also to derived rules. This was already touched on in Section 5. The point here is that we are imagining that (*C to R*) is not even a derived rule of English.

[88] This does not implicitly appeal to metaphysical modality. Any appeal is only to natural laws, nothing more. My overall position is even compatible with taking natural laws as primitive, and then using them to characterize a *factual* notion of physical or natural modality; see Maudlin (2007) for this type of approach. This is related to why synthetic *a priority* can also be robust, though the issue is subtle.

as well say that naming your son "God" allows you to establish the existence of God. This is silly; adding such rules for deploying "God" changes what is meant by "God"-involving sentences. And most of these alternative meanings will be completely irrelevant to claims about God *in our current language.*

The meaning-based approach to the *a priori* covers all that we want covered and nothing else. It does not force us to say that all *a priori* claims are analytic, only that robust *a priori* warrant is rooted, directly or indirectly, in our mastery of meanings. Nor does it force us to say that all *a priori* truths are necessary, only that when we have *a priori* warrant for believing a contingency, it is because our linguistic rules set up a connection between the guise under which it is known and the facts, so that the sentence cannot reasonably fail to express a truth, even if what it expresses is contingent.

And when necessary truths are known *a priori*, those truths must be, in a certain sense, metaphysically soft. There is no chance of gaining substantive, guise-independent knowledge of the world by way of our meanings alone. I will discuss this further in the final section (Section 9). Before doing so, I want to defend the meaning-based theory of the *a priori* by answering powerful philosophical challenges both to robust *a priority* (Section 7) and to the importance of the *a priori*/*a posteriori* distinction itself (Section 8).

7 Defending Robust *A Priority*

The meaning-based theory of the *a priori* delivers a standard notion of *a priori* truth. It also delivers robust *a priority*. This involves warrant that does not depend on experience and is also impossible to directly undermine with further experiences or new empirical evidence.

This aligns with what all of us actually expect, at least outside of the philosophy room. Nobody has ever worried that the Hubble telescope's observations might provide evidence for or against classical logic. Nobody has ever lost one night of sleep concerned that the particle accelerator at CERN might produce experimental results that could establish or refute Goldbach's conjecture.[89] It is not just that we think such outcomes are unlikely. It's instead that the very idea of having empirical evidence for or against these claims borders on incoherence. This is crucial. While some philosophers still denounce the *a priori* from their pulpits, they rarely practice what they preach.

This seems compelling, but there is a powerful counterpoint drawn from intellectual history. For hundreds of years the truths of Euclidean geometry were popular examples of *a priori* truths that would never and could never be overturned by experience. Yet the supposedly impossible is now actual. Non-Euclidean

---

[89] A similar example is given in the introduction to Boghossian and Peacocke (2000).

geometries were developed in the nineteenth century in mathematics and in the early twentieth century the Euclidean view of physical space was supplanted, when Einstein's general theory of relativity overtook Newtonian universal gravitation as our favored theory of space(time).[90] We now reasonably believe that the geometry of physical space is Non-Euclidean.[91] At first glance, this supposedly robust *a priori* theory *par excellence* was not robustly *a priori*, so maybe it's reasonable to conclude that nothing else is either.

The canonical response to this is simple: we must distinguish between pure and applied geometry. Pure geometry is a discipline of mathematics, entirely *a priori*, in a robust sense. Applied geometry is not; it instead concerns physical space. Pure and applied geometry were not always clearly distinguished in pre-nineteenth-century discussions. When this knot is untangled, it's clear that it was a mistake to ever think that applied geometry was *a priori*. So goes the canonical response.

This response is quite simple. It's probably too simple, in a number of ways, but the gist of it is difficult to contest. Applying pure mathematics to the physical world requires bridge principles – principles that directly connect the mathematical with the physical. Bridge principles are neither purely mathematical nor purely non-mathematical; instead they are mixed, by their very nature. From our modern perspective, choices between them are governed by little more than expediency. If some of our bridge principles stop being useful, we abandon them freely, with glad hearts. This perspective easily recovers for us the very natural result that pure mathematics is completely insulated from empirical confirmation and disconfirmation.

An alternative perspective was provided by W. V. Quine in the mid-twentieth century, by building on various discussions of underdetermination from the philosophy of science literature. Quine argued that because the sentences in our overall theory of the world face experience together, rather than individually, *any* portion of our conceptual scheme is in principle revisable in the face of experience. Take the case of physical geometry again. Rather than giving up our bridge laws in light of experience, we could have instead altered our pure geometric principles, or even our logic. There are many different ways of making our overall theory of the world compatible with the totality of our experiences, so nothing is safe. This is Quine's holism argument. There are serious questions about how the argument and Quine's position work in detail, but the overall vision is seductive.[92]

---

[90] See Gray (1989) and Maudlin (2012) for accounts.

[91] This is not to say that realism about physical space and its geometry is forced by modern science; see Sklar (1974) for an overview of these issues.

[92] For some questions and challenges, see Colyvan (2006) and Wright (1986).

A common interpretation sees Quine as rejecting the (robust) *a priori* entirely.[93] But the common interpretation is wrong: Quine was not arguing against robust *a priority*. We only think he was because we translate Quine's argument into terms he would not accept. Quine's position is only that any *sentence* can be revised to accommodate experience. He explicitly and consistently conceives of our conceptual scheme in a syntactic, sentence-based manner. Understood in this way, Quine's thesis is not very radical. Few have ever denied it. Not even Carnap, who Quine is seen as challenging on this exact point.[94]

As was stressed in Section 5 when discussing the translation mistake, to understand robust *a priority* as concerning sentences trivializes the notion. To turn Quine's argument into a substantive disavowal of the robust *a priori*, we need an added premise stating that the meanings of the relevant sentences are retained across revisions. Since Quine's claims are completely general, this would amount to the premise that *any* revision in our attitudes toward sentences is compatible with those sentences retaining their meaning. So you could even start using the word "not" as a name for your dog without changing its meaning. Obviously, this is absurd. Accepting it is tantamount to giving up on *any* recognizable notion of meaning. Quine himself was happy to do just that. His modern-day followers are not. This crucial difference leads many contemporary philosophers to misunderstand Quine's position.

In his own words, Quine's argument concerns not meaning, but constraints on proper translations. Put in terms of translation, Quine's holism argument only works against the robust *a priori* if we add the premise that no differences in our attitudes toward sentences undermine homophonic translation – translation of each sentence into itself, across the revision. If this is right, then our uses of "not" at any earlier time translate into our uses of "not" now, even if we have drastically changed our attitudes toward and usage of sentences involving "not" in the meantime. With this added premise, we now have a Quine-style argument against robust *a priority*, at least if these changes are rational. But this argument is not one that Quine accepted – in his writings he *explicitly* and *consistently* denies this additional premise.

This is well known, even somewhat infamous. In various places, Quine argued that when you change your logic, you change the subject. So those who seemingly deny our basic logical principles, like the law of noncontradiction, should not be translated as doing so.[95] Yes, *Quine* argued for this most

---

[93] This interpretation was pioneered in Putnam (1976). It interprets Quine as offering an ineffective circularity argument in the first four sections of "Two Dogmas," and an effective and distinct confirmation holism argument in the last two sections.

[94] See page 318 of Carnap (1937).

[95] At greatest length in Quine (1970). Quine's argument is cleaned up and extended in Warren (2018).

Carnapian of theses. For those of us who accept meanings it is a very short step from this to the claim that if you change your logic, you change the meanings of some of your logical expressions. Sometimes Quine's endorsement of this argument is treated as a slip or a late change of mind, but it was not. Quine gave this argument many times, never wavering from it.[96] It is not a slip, but instead a central aspect of his philosophy. So Quine is not actually an opponent of the robust *a priori* at all. Yet another bit of philosophical folklore turns out false.

Of course, exegesis is less important than philosophy. So forget what Quine thought. Some philosophers and physicists have actually argued that it is rational to revise our basic logical principles in light of the discoveries of empirical science, quantum mechanics in particular. The most prominent and sustained case for this was made by Hilary Putnam. Putnam argued that making sense of quantum mechanics rationally requires revisions to classical logic in favor of so-called quantum logic.[97] Quantum logic alters some of the distribution laws (from "*p* and (*q* or *r*)" deduce "(*p* and *q*) or (*p* and *r*)") in classical logic, but the precise formal details aren't important here. We start with *a priori* warrant for accepting the principles of classical logic. Putnam argued that this warrant was defeated, directly, by empirical information. If correct, this shows that our *a priori* warrant for accepting logical principles is not robust.

With the benefit of hindsight, we know that Putnam's empirical case for quantum logic failed. The proposal itself was never really worked out in detail, didn't seem to work for its intended purpose, and was based on little more than a loose mathematical analogy.[98] Putnam himself later abandoned it.[99] In a sense, this doesn't really matter. The mere coherence of Putnam's case puts pressure on the robust *a priority* of logic, and similar cases – whether actual or not – put pressure on robust *a priority* across the board.

I hate to be a broken record, but my response to this appeals to the translation mistake. Meaning-based theorists are not and never have been saying that experiences cannot cause a revision in logic or mathematics. They are instead saying that these revisions involve *arational* meaning change. To undermine robust *a priority*, we need experience to undermine our *a priori* warrant for accepting a claim, not a sentence. At the very least, this requires having an attitude toward the very same claim both before and after the revision. The use-based metasemantics accepted by meaning-based theorists entails that so-called quantum logicians are not disagreeing with us, but are instead operating with similar but different logical concepts.

---

[96] A version of the argument is in section 13 of Quine (1960).   [97] In Putnam (1968).
[98] See Maudlin (2005).   [99] See Putnam (2005).

This move is metasemantically well-motivated, but some philosophers are suspicious of it. In particular, Timothy Williamson, in his case against "understanding-assent" links.[100] Applied to the case at hand, Williamson argues that Putnam, as an expert logician, understands logical notions as well as anyone does. This is true enough. Putnam was a world-class logician; he even significantly contributed to the resolution of Hilbert's tenth problem. His expert status is supposed to block the response that he doesn't understand the logical notions in question.

It does sound silly and arrogant to say that Putnam did not "understand" disjunction, conjunction, or other basic logical notions. Yet the trouble here is only that the word "understand" and its associations are being leveraged. I agree that Putnam understood *something* with his words "or" and "and." But that is not the claim needed for the argument against robust *a priority*; the claim needed is instead that *Putnam understands these words exactly as we do*. That is not established by Putnam's status as an expert logician. We should drop the "understanding" terminology and focus on whether or not the deviant expert *means what we mean* by the crucial terms, or, if you prefer, whether they have the *same concepts* that we do.

Would it matter if Putnam insisted that he meant the same thing by "or" and "and" that we do? Not particularly. Meaning is determined by use, it is not under the direct control of intention or stipulation. And even if Putnam has some kind of privileged access to what he means by "or" and "and," he doesn't have privileged access to what *we* mean by "or" and "and." His claims about metasemantics and translation are not privileged; rejecting them is not disrespectful, nor does it undermine his status as an expert.[101]

Not only can meaning-based theorists argue *that* meaning has changed in the quantum logic case, they can say *how* it has changed – if Putnam really reasons according to the principles of quantum logic, then he will have moved from a classical language to a language in which the meanings of "or" and "and" vindicate the principles of quantum logic. This is because, according to inferentialists and implicit definition theorists, what Putnam means by "or" and "and" is determined by how he uses "or" and "and," and – by assumption – he uses them according to the principles of quantum logic. We can say this even without fully translating the quantum logician's language into our own.

We thus end near where we began. We must allow the universal revisability of *sentences*, but we should not let this lead us into a sloppy simplicity about theory

---

[100] See Williamson (2007) for the argument and Warren (2021) for a full response. A different recipe to the same purpose was given in Casalegno (2004) – Williamson endorses this recipe as well in several of his contributions to Boghossian and Williamson (2020).

[101] See also 7.V of Warren (2020).

change. Once we add realistic nuances about how distinct sentences differentially relate to each other, to experience, and to how we treat revisions of them with respect to meaning change, a more sophisticated picture emerges. This picture allows universal revisability over sentences but not over claims or statements or propositions or content. Sentence revisions are not all on a semantic and epistemological par.[102]

This is important, since opponents of robust *a priori* sometimes suggest or hint or insinuate that they are in a struggle against dogmatists. The thought is that we friends of robust *a priori* have foreclosed on certain avenues of deliberation in advance. Such foreclosures risk locking us into immature conceptual choices. I agree that conceptual dogmatism is practically unwise, but it is a mistake to think that accepting robust *a priori* amounts to dogmatism. I encourage everyone to freely develop alternative logical and mathematical systems. I would happily start using one of these new systems if I could, were doing so the best option for me, practically speaking and all things considered. There is no dogmatism here; let a thousand flowers bloom. Take a swim in the boundless ocean of unlimited possibilities.

In fact, the tables can be turned. I accuse opponents of robust *a priori* not of dogmatism, but of holding fast to a metasemantics that hinders progress. It hinders progress by pushing us toward thinking that merely practical matters are factual. We shouldn't waste time arguing about which logical or mathematical theory is *really correct*, from God's point of view. We should instead evaluate alternative logics and alternative mathematical systems in a thoroughly *practical* fashion.[103] Blurring the line between practical and descriptive issues sidetracks us with pointless artifactual questions. Questions like: is the law of noncontradiction *really true*? Are the distribution laws *really true*? To ask these questions is as silly as asking, when considering a revision to the rules of chess, which chess-like rules are *really* correct? To think that these are matters of objective fact is to implicitly accept a heavyweight metaphysics that we should all reject in the strongest terms.[104]

8 *A Priori* in the Epistemological Joints

Recently a novel form of skepticism about the *a priori* has been pushed by some epistemological externalists.[105] These skeptics do not deny the existence of a distinction between *a priori* and *a posteriori* knowledge, they instead argue that the distinction is epistemologically unimportant.

---

[102] See Friedman (2000) for an account of how this works in cases of scientific theory change.
[103] This is basically the principle of tolerance advocated in Carnap (1937).
[104] See Warren (2016) for some relevant arguments.
[105] See Hawthorne (2007) and Williamson (2007) for early claims in this direction.

Proponents often put this vividly by saying the *a priori/a posteriori* distinction does not cut at the epistemological joints. We can treat this way of talking as a mere metaphor.[106] Epistemology concerns norms of belief formation. Many epistemological distinctions are of significance to us, for instance the distinctions between knowing something versus merely believing it and between being justified in believing something versus not being justified in believing it. The suggestion here is that even if the *a priori* versus *a posteriori* distinction can coherently be drawn, it is not important to our epistemological theorizing in the way these other distinctions are.

The most developed argument for this is from Williamson.[107] He gives an example meant to show that there are clear cases of *a priori* knowing so similar to clear cases of *a posteriori* knowing that the significance of the distinction is called into question. Williamson's example concerns Norman coming to know two different claims:

(1) All crimson things are red
(2) All recent volumes of *Who's Who* are red

Claim (1) is supposed to be a clear case of an *a priori* truth and claim (2) a clear case of an *a posteriori* truth. You might already feel some uneasiness about this, but let's press forward. Williamson tells stories about Norman's knowledge of these claims. To set up his stories, he stipulates that in learning the word "crimson," Norman did not learn any rule connecting it to "red," like my (*C to R*) rule from Section 6. Let's suppose that Norman learned the words "crimson" and "red" in completely disconnected circumstances.

Williamson's stories run as follows. In coming to know (1), Norman imagines a representative example of crimson, and then exercises his skill in applying the term "red" to judge it red. Since he made no additional assumptions about the imagined object, he generalizes to conclude (1). Assuming this imaginative process was sufficiently skillful, we should say that on its basis Norman comes to know (1). In coming to know (2), Norman imagines a representative example of a recent volume of *Who's Who*, and then exercises his skill in applying the term "red" to judge it red. Since he made no additional assumptions about the imagined object, he generalizes to conclude (1). Assuming this imaginative process was sufficiently skillful, we should say that, on its basis, Norman comes to know (2).

In neither case did Norman call upon episodic memories or particular bits of empirical information. His knowledge in both cases was generated by a use of

---

[106] For a nonmetaphorical spelling out of joint-carving talk, see Sider (2011).
[107] In Williamson (2013).

imagination together with a sufficiently skillful application of the concept of red, which Norman has, by assumption, mastered. This story is most naturally told within an externalist, knowledge-first framework of the kind Williamson is well-known for developing.[108] But that framework isn't strictly required. We could also make the point in terms of Norman's *a priori* warrant in each of these cases being sufficient for knowledge of (1) and (2) given the factual situation.[109] If we insist, we can count his knowledge of (1) as *a priori* and his knowledge of (2) as *a posteriori*, but the differences between these two pieces of knowledge are relatively superficial, given the close similarity of the cognitive processes that generate them. From this, Williamson concludes that the distinction does not cut at the epistemological joints.

There are two ways to read Williamson's argument. The extreme way claims that (1) and (2) are *representative*. The argument's conclusion is then that there is no epistemologically important difference between any examples of the *a priori* and the *a posteriori*. Williamson suggests the extreme reading by arguing that both (1) and (2) are relevantly similar to canonical cases of *a priori* and *a posteriori* knowledge, respectively.

The response to the extreme version of the argument is obvious: neither (1) nor (2) is representative. Given Williamson's stipulations about the case, claim (1) is at best a synthetic *a priori* truth. Many proponents of the *a priori* reject this category altogether. Given this, it is starkly question-begging to take this example of a disputed case as representative of the *a priori*. Claim (2) is even worse as a representative example of the *a posteriori*, since it involves a generalization that is, by stipulation, not drawing on previous experiences. Both (1) and (2) are very special cases; they have obviously been chosen to be similar to each other. Hard cases make bad law. Williamson has hand-picked special, non-representative examples. Given this, nothing interesting and general about the relationship between the *a priori* and the *a posteriori* follows from his examples, whatever else we say about them.

Even still, if Norman knows (1) *a priori* and (2) *a posteriori* in the ways that Williamson describes, his argument would at least show that some cases of *a priori* knowing are relevantly similar to some cases of *a posteriori* knowing. This gives us a modest reading of the argument. The conclusion now is only that the line between the two categories is not drawn in an epistemologically principled way. We could imagine a similar argument about the legal distinction between felonies and misdemeanors. If some felonies are morally indistinguishable from some misdemeanors, then it is impossible to argue that the line

---

[108] In Williamson (2000).

[109] Boghossian (2020a) argues that if set up using (in my terms) warrant, Williamson's claims implicitly assume a reliabilist theory of warrant.

between them always tracks some morally significant joint.[110] The conclusion of this modest reading of the argument falls far short of the conclusion of the extreme reading, but it is not without interest.

Fortunately, the modest conclusion also doesn't follow. Even granting his story about (1) – something that is by no means without problems of its own – Williamson's account of Norman's knowledge of (2) fails. To see this, first imagine an analogous case. Suppose that you ask me whether all members of the Stanford philosophy department have dark hair. One thing I certainly would *not* do, in attempting to answer this question, would be to imagine a generic, dark-haired member of the Stanford philosophy department, use my skill in applying the complex predicate "has dark hair," and then generalize to conclude that all members of the Stanford philosophy department have dark hair. That would be laughable and epistemologically irrelevant. Yet it is on a par with Williamson's story about (2) if all members of the Stanford philosophy department, in fact, have dark hair.

Others have also responded to Williamson by rejecting his account of Norman's knowledge of (2). Some committed internalists have suggested that for Norman to know (2) in anything like this fashion, he must antecedently know that all recent volumes of *Who's Who* have the same color.[111] This adds an extra, inferential step to Williamson's story about Norman's knowledge. Williamson has replied by rejecting the internalism built into this reply. He seems to suspect that any way of rejecting his story will assume an objectionably strong form of internalism.[112] But we don't need to make any internalist move to reject Williamson's account of Norman's knowledge of (2).

The crucial difference between Norman's two described acts of imagination concerns the way imagination interacts with the content of the supposition. With (1), Norman simply imagines a qualitatively red thing. With (2), qualitative imagining is not enough. There must also be some additional source of content to distinguish imagining a genuine volume of *Who's Who* from imagining a qualitatively indistinguishable fake. To see this, consider imagining a qualitative duplicate of a recent volume of *Who's Who*. By hypothesis, imagining the ersatz volume of *Who's Who* is qualitatively indistinguishable from imagining the genuine volume. Yet these two imaginative acts have different content, so there must be a source of content that goes beyond the qualitative. In the case of (2), the particular qualitative features imagined were not required by the supposition. In logical terms, they play the role of auxiliary premises about the imagined object.

---

[110] This example was suggested by Yu Guo.   [111] See Boghossian (2020a).
[112] See Williamson (2020b).

This is where the fallacy is hiding. The logical rule of universal generalization permits us, upon establishing that an object with property F also has property G, to conclude that *everything* that is F is also G *only* when we have made no special assumptions about the object beyond its being F. I know that Mickey Mouse can talk, on this basis I cannot validly conclude that all mice can talk. A version of this mistake is made in Williamson's story about Norman's knowledge of (2). Norman imagined a recent volume of *Who's Who* via imaginative stipulation, adding in imagination that said volume has a certain, particular qualitative appearance. This goes beyond the starting supposition. Norman then uses this auxiliary information to conclude that the imagined book is red, not the information required by the antecedent stipulation. In effect, Norman illicitly uses an auxiliary premise in his reasoning. So Norman's reasoning to (2) commits the equivalent of a logical fallacy of generalization. Williamson's story fails because in it Norman's reasoning embodies a logical fallacy in a disguised form. So Norman might be able to know (1) in the way Williamson suggests, but not (2).[113]

This criticism does not require skepticism about gaining knowledge – even knowledge about the physical world – through imagination. This is important, since Williamson has recently been developing an interesting cognitive approach to the uses of imagination in epistemology.[114] I am not hostile to that approach. My criticism of Norman's knowledge of (2) does not apply to all attempts to gain knowledge using imagination; it concerns the generalization step in Norman's reasoning. Using imagination to skillfully simulate particular objects and circumstances does not involve a broad generalization step. It's plausible that when imagination is employed in a default, reality-oriented mode, in order to simulate the world as an aid to planning, information drawn from many empirical sources is recruited to play a role in the reasoning. This makes a certain recognizable class of knowing by imagining *a posteriori,* and there is no direct parallel between this *a posteriori* method of knowing by imagining and our *a priori* methods.

Williamson's case against the importance of the *a priori/a posteriori* distinction is flawed in both general and particular ways. Obviously, rebutting an argument that a distinction is *not* important does not thereby show that the distinction *is* important. But Williamson already made his job easier by focusing only on *a priori* warrant that came from generalizing on the basis of imagination. His case didn't even attempt to touch robust *a priori* warrant, which is of clear and natural epistemological importance. So even if

---

[113] Actually I don't even think he can come to know (1) in Williamson's way; see Section 6 for a more plausible story about knowledge of (1).

[114] See Williamson (2016), building on some of the work in Williamson (2007).

Williamson's argument had worked against its intended target, we could still take robust *a priority* to be of crucial epistemological importance. The notion of *a priority* delivered by meaning-based theories cuts at the epistemological joints. This Element's final section will – indirectly and implicitly – strengthen the case for this, by stepping back to reflect on the nature of epistemology and epistemic evaluations.

9 The Nature of Epistemology

This Element started with an overview of epistemic evaluations (Section 1). The main point of that overview was to fix on some terminology, but there I also claimed that our epistemic practices served to track and communicate about epistemic norms. These norms concern epistemic rights and duties to have or not have particular beliefs in particular situations, and to employ or not employ certain belief-forming methods in certain circumstances.

This is what epistemic evaluations *do*. They are epistemic score-keeping tools that allow us to enforce our distinctively epistemic norms. I don't think this stance is likely to be controversial. Yet accepting it leaves lingering many philosophical questions about the nature of epistemic evaluations. Answering some of these questions sheds further light on the *a priori/a posteriori* distinction itself, so I close with a foray into meta-epistemology.

There are usually facts about whether our beliefs are true or false. There are also facts about whether a given belief-forming method is reliable, and whether it would be reliable in alternative situations. There is a ton indeterminacy here, and not just on the margins. I'll discuss that in a moment. But in an ordinary sense, there are often facts about truth and reliability. We don't always have access to these facts, but they are visible from the God's eye point of view (to speak metaphorically).

Yet *we* form beliefs and use belief-forming methods looking not from the God's eye point of view but instead out from the inside of our primate skulls. There are many ways for beliefs to be false and for belief-forming methods to go wrong that can't always be sussed out from the inside. Sometimes what went wrong is even entirely *outside of us*, even apart from first-person access. A crucial part of our epistemic practices concerns recognizing this and working around it. Yet we shouldn't try to work around it in ways that eschew the connection of epistemology to true beliefs and reliable methods. To do that is to burn down the externalist forest in order to preserve the internalist trees.

Our epistemic norms come packaged in many different forms, but truth and reliability are never too far from our epistemic concerns. To say this is *not* to thereby accept a form of reliabilism about warrant. The basic idea of reliabilism is that warrant is generated by forming a belief using a reliable method. In its simplest form, reliabilism says that beliefs are warranted if and only if they are formed using reliable methods.[115] While I agree that reliability is of crucial importance, reducing warrant to reliability and nothing else is undesirable. Doing so risks losing sight of the evident fact that talk of "reliability" is shot through with indeterminacy and painted over by our interests. Just how reliable must a method be to count as "reliable"? Over what space of alternatives must it be reliable? What if a method is perfectly reliable, so that it always leads to true beliefs, but is so slow that it is practically useless? How do we trade reliability off against other costs? What of perfectly reliable but opaque methods, like the method of believing Fermat's last theorem (used in 1950)? I could go on and on.[116] For these and other reasons, we can't analyze all of our epistemic notions in terms of reliability, and even those we can so-analyze inherit more than a bit of fuzziness.

In an important series of papers on the *a priori*, Hartry Field used points like these to support *non-factualism* in epistemology.[117] Epistemic nonfactualists reject epistemic facts altogether. They argue that epistemic sentences are semantically expressive – they merely express our attitudes, without making any descriptive claims.[118] I agree with the the spirit of Field's nonfactualist position, but not its letter. I think that epistemic claims are factual, except on the margins, but they aren't *perfectly objective*, at least in one sense of that term. Given what we mean by "knowledge," "justification," and the like, saying that someone knows something, or is justified in believing it, is a descriptive, factual claim. It can be true or false. Yet this point is compatible with thinking that epistemic notions are tightly connected to our epistemic evaluations, and that our epistemic evaluations – and our epistemic concepts themselves – are shaped and molded by our goals, interests, and priorities.

So unlike Field, I don't think we need an expressivist semantics to do justice to our epistemic evaluations.[119] An expressivist semantics tries to build a semantic theory that allows certain sentences to merely express attitudes, rather than describe the world. I don't think this is needed. Even if we reject expressivism, there is still room to distinguish between our epistemic concepts and the world that they apply to. Describing the world *in language* always allows the factoring of our descriptive claims into both linguistic and worldly components.[120]

---

[115] For reliabilism see Goldman (1979); see Bonjour (1980) for a famous critique.

[116] For a detailed related discussion, see Field (2000). See also Berry (2019).

[117] Field (1996, 1998, 2000, 2005).   [118] See Field (1994, 2000).

[119] Field (1994) argued for adapting Gibbard's (1990) quasi-realist semantic framework; see Blackburn (1984) for the origination of this sort of approach.

[120] In fact, Einheuser's (2006) framework for this is, like Gibbard's (1990) normative framework, a modal semantics where "worlds" are pairs.

Likewise for concepts. The claim that René is warranted in believing that 2+2=4 connects up to an attitude of approval toward René's epistemic actions. It also connects up to various norms of belief and belief formation. But it is overkill to rewrite standard semantics to make sense of these connections. Worse, doing so risks confusing the semantic with the metasemantic, and application to the world with other aspects of a concept's conceptual role.

There are better ways to recognize that epistemology connects up with our goals and practices. One way involves always keeping in mind that our epistemic standards and practices are *not uniquely correct*. Slightly different collections of epistemic concepts would have led to very similar practices. Many such alternative practices would be no worse than our own, even when evaluated by our standards. There is more than one way to skin an epistemic cat. Some alternative practices might use variants of our key epistemic concepts – knowledge, warrant, and so on. While others might use totally alien concepts for similar purposes. Such imagined practices are not *our* practices, but they may be as good or even better, in practical terms. Of course, not every apparently "epistemic" practice is truly *epistemic*, by our lights. Some imagined "epistemic" practices simply give up too much. If an alternative practice of evaluating beliefs showed no concern at all for truth or reliability, we wouldn't count that practice as "epistemic." Likewise if the supposedly epistemic terms had no connection to the practice's epistemic norms. In a strict sense, only our practice's evaluations count as *epistemic* evaluations. In a loose sense, any sufficiently similar alternative practice would also count as "epistemic" or at least as *epistemic-like*.[121]

None of this means that our usual epistemic claims are not factual. Very similar but less sweeping points can also be made about our concept of a chair or even our basic concept of an object.[122] An alien language might not count chairs made out of metal as "chairs," or they might talk as if objects can be radically spatiotemporally discontinuous. Alien languages need not share our conceptual scheme even when they can talk about all of the same facts, in a coarse-grained sense. This does not imply that our claims about chairs and objects are nonfactual, so the analogous points don't imply that our claims about warrant and knowledge are nonfactual either.

Our practices of epistemic evaluation play an incredibly important practical role in our lives. If an alternative practice's notions and norms were better able to serve our practical goals, all things considered, we'd have practical – *not epistemic* – reasons for switching over and making that alternative practice our

---

[121] This and other forms of conceptual pluralism can be spelled out more precisely; see Warren (2015a, chapter 5 of 2020).

[122] Something like this is the central claim of quantifier variance; see Hirsch and Warren (2019) for an introduction.

own. Our epistemological practices are not unique, even structurally. So while our epistemic claims are factual, in a soft sense, our epistemology need not be uniquely correct, from God's point of view.

This is also compatible with there being firm factual constraints on any belief-forming methods that count as warrant generating. While rejecting simplistic forms of reliabilism, we must also, as I have stressed, admit that epistemology, by its very nature, is intimately concerned with truth and reliability. So it is plausible to reject reliabilist analyses of warrant while also thinking that when we're reliable about some subject, epistemology must be able to explain said reliability. Hardcore versions of realism in acausal subjects violate this constraint, making it difficult to accept realist theories while also thinking us reliable about these subjects.[123]

The problem isn't only about explaining our reliability. In most subjects, we think we are entitled to some of our beliefs. We also think that some of our beliefs are justified. Some of them might even count as knowledge. All of these notions – explicable reliability, entitlement, justification, knowledge – plausibly require *connections* of some kind between our beliefs and the facts. Each respective notion might require a different connection than do the other notions, but without any connection at all between our beliefs and the facts, mediated and maintained by our belief-forming methods, epistemic achievement would be impossible. And if connections are shunned, epistemic achievement becomes possible, but only at the cost of being worthless.

Epistemic goodness, in all of its forms, requires connections between facts and beliefs. Epistemologists can and should continue to argue about the strength and nature of these connections, for each respective epistemic notion. Many philosophical theories of supposedly *a priori* subjects (mathematics, logic, ethics) make such connections impossible, provided we stay within the broad confines of modern science's account of human cognition. This is another point that has made the *a priori* itself a bit suspect – a vague feeling that no reasonable epistemology is possible in supposedly *a priori* domains.

Notice though that this trouble only arises if a hardcore form of metaphysical realism is assumed in these domains. According to this form of realism, mathematics, logic, and ethics are *about* free-standing, mind-independent, non-physical, factual domains. If you assume this, no reasonable epistemology is possible for mathematics, logic, or ethics. What are your options then? It seems you must *either* implausibly connect our physical brains to this noncausal realm (see Section 4), *or* give up on reliability in these areas, *or* say that we are reliable

---

[123] See the discussion in the introduction to Field (1989), building on Benacerraf (1973). See also Warren (2017).

only by way of a cosmic fluke. All of these options are extremely unappealing. It is far, far better and simpler to give up on hardcore realism in *a priori* domains.

Let's *modus tollens* this *modus ponens*. The meaning-based theory of the *a priori* I have offered provides a reasonable epistemology in these areas. It manages this by eschewing metaphysical realism in these domains. The truths in *a priori* domains are lightweight. Nothing but shadows of our practices of reasoning and using language, understood syntactically. One might even call them "shadows of syntax." In fact, somebody already did: *me*.[124] The story becomes a bit more involved for certain challenge cases, but as we've seen (Section 6), a meaning-based theory is widely applicable. If the truths in mathematics (for example) are merely shadows of our syntactic practices, then connections between the truths and our beliefs are abundant and easy to find. At bottom, this is why and how meaning-based theories of the *a priori* allow for explainable reliability, entitlement, justification, and knowledge in traditional *a priori* domains.

Anyone who accepts a meaning-based theory of *a priori* warrant should accept a lightweight metaphysics in order to have a satisfying overall theory.[125] In some noncausal subject areas, like logic and mathematics, we certainly seem to have *a priori* warrant and *a priori* knowledge. If we want to accept these appearances without also accepting magic, the meaning-based approach is the only game in town. So we have two options left to us. We either accept the meaning-based approach or go with the Quineans and leave the *a priori* behind. Every other strategy ends up appealing to magic at some crucial point.

The rejection of hardcore metaphysical realism in *a priori* domains is, as they say, a feature, not a bug. The analogy between the physical world and the "world" of logic and mathematics is overblown. We access these "worlds" easily, in an *a priori* way, because the worlds themselves are reflections of our practices. They are domains of fact, they are utterly necessary, but their factuality is soft, not hard, and their necessity is projected, not found. To fully embrace this approach is to accept a form of what used to be called <u>conventionalism</u> in these areas. This was the favored theory of science-inspired philosophers in the early to mid-twentieth century. It was later almost universally rejected, but mainly for reasons that we can now see through. If we take a sensible, conventionalist view of logic and mathematics, then we can have the *a priori*, in a strong form, without mystery or magic.

Our practices of making epistemic evaluations are some of the most important human practices. These practices have both internalist and externalist strands, and for good reason too. We want our methods to be safe and reliable, but we are unable

---

[124] In Warren (2020).

[125] Boghossian attempted to deny this in his papers on the epistemology of logic, but he has been criticized for this; for example, see Williamson (2020a).

to take an external perspective on ourselves. When we consider our split notion of warrant, we see that both the externalist aspect and the internalist aspect sometimes do and sometimes don't depend upon experience in an epistemically relevant way. And in some cases, the warrant that isn't gained by way of experience can't be lost by way of experience either. It is impossible to fully understand our epistemic evaluations and practices without understanding this. In other words, we can't understand *ourselves* without understanding the *a priori*, without magic.

References

Alston, William P. (1988). "The Deontological Concept of Epistemic Justification." *Philosophical Perspectives* 2: 257–299.

Ayer, Alfred J (1940). *The Foundations of Empirical Knowledge*. London: Macmillan.

Ayer, Alfred J. (1946). *Language, Truth, and Logic*, 2nd ed. London: Victor Gollancz.

Bealer, George. (2000). "A Theory of the A Priori." *Pacific Philosophical Quarterly* 81(1): 1–30.

Beaumont, Bertrand. (1954). "Hegel and the Seven Planets." *Mind* 63(250): 246–248.

Beebe, James R. (2009). "The Abductivist Reply to Skepticism." *Philosophy and Phenomenological Research* 79(3): 605–636.

Belnap, Nuel. (1962). "Tonk, Plonk, and Plink." *Analysis* 22(6): 130–134.

Benacerraf, Paul. (1973). "Mathematical Truth." *Journal of Philosophy* 70(19): 661–679.

Bengson, John. (2015). "The Intellectual Given." *Mind* 124(495): 707–760.

Bennett, Jonathan. (1966). *Kant's Analytic*. Cambridge: Cambridge University Press.

Bennett, Jonathan. (1971). *Locke, Berkeley, Hume: Central Themes*. Oxford: Oxford University Press.

Berry, Sharon. (2019). "External World Skepticism, Confidence and Psychologism about the Problem of Priors." *Southern Journal of Philosophy* 57(3): 324–346.

Blackburn, Simon. (1984). *Spreading the Word: Groundings in the Philosophy of Language*. Oxford: Clarendon Press.

Boghossian, Paul. (1996). "Analyticity." *Nous* 30: 360–391.

Boghossian, Paul. (2000). "Knowledge of Logic." In Paul Boghossian and Christopher Peacocke (eds.), *New Essays on the A Priori*. Oxford: Oxford University Press: 229–254.

Boghossian, Paul. (2001). "How are Objective Epistemic Reasons Possible?" *Philosophical Studies* 106: 1–40.

Boghossian, Paul. (2003). "Blind Reasoning." *Proceeding of the Aristotelian Society: Supplementary Volume* 77: 225–248.

Boghossian, Paul. (2014). "What is Inference?" *Philosophical Studies* 169(1): 1–18.

Boghossian, Paul. (2020a). "Do We Have Reason to Doubt the Importance of the Distinction between A Priori and A Posteriori Knowledge? A Reply to

Williamson." In Boghossian and Williamson (eds.), *Debating the A Priori*. Oxford: Oxford University Press: 137–155.

Boghossian, Paul. (2020b). "Intuition, Understanding, and the a Priori." In Boghossian and Williamson, *Debating the a Priori*. Oxford: Oxford University Press: 186–207.

Boghossian, Paul and Christopher Peacocke, eds. (2000). *New Essays on the A Priori*. Oxford: Oxford University Press.

Boghossian, Paul and Timothy Williamson. (2020). *Debating the A Priori*. Oxford: Oxford University Press.

Bonjour, Laurence. (1980). "Externalist Theories of Empirical Knowledge." *Midwest Studies in Philosophy* 5: 53–73.

Bonjour, Laurence. (1998). *In Defense of Pure Reason*. Cambridge: Cambridge University Press.

Bradley, Darren. (forthcoming). "Objective Bayesianism and the Abductivist Reply to Scepticism." *Episteme*.

Burge, Tyler. (1993). "Content Preservation." *Philosophical Review* 102(4): 457–488.

Burge, Tyler. (2000). "Frege on Apriority." In Paul Boghossian and Christopher Peacocke (eds.), *New Essays on the A Priori*. Oxford: Oxford University Press: 11–42.

Cappelen, Herman. (2012). *Philosophy without Intuitions*. Oxford: Oxford University Press.

Carnap, Rudolf. (1937). *The Logical Syntax of Language*. London: Routledge and Kegan Paul.

Carnap, Rudolf. (1950). "Empiricism, Semantics, and Ontology." *Revue Internationale de Philosophie* 4(11): 20–40.

Carnap, Rudolf. (1962). *Logical Foundations of Probability*, 2nd ed. Chicago: University of Chicago Press.

Casalegno, Paolo. (2004). "Logical Concepts and Logical Inferences." *Dialectica* 58: 395–411.

Casullo, Albert. (2003). *A Priori Justification*. Oxford: Oxford University Press.

Chalmers, David J. (2012). *Constructing the World*. Oxford: Oxford University Press.

Chisholm, Rodrick. (1977). "The Truths of Reason." In *Theory of Knowledge*, 2nd ed. Englewood Cliffs: Prentice Hall: 34–61.

Chudnoff, Elijah. (2013). *Intuition*. Oxford: Oxford University Press.

Coffa, J. Alberto. (1991). *The Semantic Tradition from Kant to Carnap: To the Vienna Station*. Cambridge: Cambridge University Press.

Colyvan, Mark. (2006). "Naturalism and the Paradox of Revisability." *Pacific Philosophical Quarterly* 87(1): 1–11.

Dennett, Daniel. (1976). "Are Dreams Experiences?" *Philosophical Review* 85(2): 151–171.

Einheuser, Iris. (2006). "Counterconventional Conditionals." *Philosophical Studies* 127(3): 459–482.

Evans, Gareth. (1979). "Reference and Contingency." *The Monist* 62(2): 161–189.

Field, Hartry. (1989). *Realism, Mathematics, & Modality.* Oxford: Basil Blackwell.

Field, Hartry. (1994). "Disquotational Truth and Factually Defective Discourse." *Philosophical Review* 103(3): 405–452.

Field, Hartry. (1996). "The A Prioricity of Logic." *Proceeding of the Aristotelian Society: New Series* 96: 359–379.

Field, Hartry. (1998). "Epistemological Nonfactualism and the A Prioricity of Logic." *Philosophical Studies* 92(1/2): 1–24.

Field, Hartry. (2000). "Apriority as an Evaluative Notion." In Paul Boghossian and Christopher Peacocke (eds.), *New Essays on the A Priori.* Oxford: Oxford University Press: 117–149.

Field, Hartry. (2005). "Recent Debates about the A Priori." In Gendler and Hawthorne (eds.), *Oxford Studies in Epistemology*, Vol. 1. Oxford: Oxford University Press: 69–88.

Fodor, Jerry A. (1981). "The Present Status of the Innateness Controversy." In *RePresentation: Philosophical Essays on the Foundations of Cognitive Science.* Cambridge, MA: The MIT Press: 257–316.

Fodor, Jerry A. (1983). *The Modularity of Mind: An Essay on Faculty Psychology.* Cambridge, MA: The MIT Press.

Franklin, James. (2001). "Resurrecting Logical Probability." *Erkenntnis* 55(2): 277–305.

Friedman, Michael. (2000). "Transcendental Philosophy and A Priori Knowledge: A Neo-Kantian Perspective." In Paul Boghossian and Christopher Peacocke (eds.), *New Essays on the A Priori.* Oxford: Oxford University Press: 367–383.

Gentzen, Gerhard. (1964). "Investigations into Logical Deduction I." *American Philosophical Quarterly* 1(4): 288–306.

Gentzen, Gerhard. (1965). "Investigations into Logical Deduction II." *American Philosophical Quarterly* 2(3): 204–218.

Gettier, Edmund L. (1963). "Is Justified True Belief Knowledge?" *Analysis* 23(6): 121–123.

Gibbard, Allan. (1990). *Wise Choices, Apt Feelings: A Theory of Normative Judgment.* Cambridge, MA: Harvard University Press.

Goldman, Alvin. (1979). "What is Justified Belief?" In Pappas (ed.), *Justification and Knowledge.* Dordrecht: D. Reidel: 1–23.

Goldman, Alvin. (1999). "A Priori Warrant and Naturalistic Epistemology: The Seventh *Philosophical Perspectives* Lecture." *Philosophical Perspectives* 13: 1–28.

Gray, Jeremy. (1989). *Ideas of Space: Euclidean, Non-Euclidean, and Relativistic*, 2nd ed. Oxford: Clarendon Press.

Harman, Gilbert. (1986). "The Meanings of Logical Constants." In Lepore (ed.), *Truth and Interpretation: Perspectives on the Philosophy of Donald Davidson*. New York: Blackwell: 125–134.

Hawthorne, John. (2002). "Deeply Contingent A Priori Knowledge." *Philosophy and Phenomenological Research* 65(2): 247–269.

Hawthorne, John. (2007). "A Priority and Externalism." In Goldberg (ed.), *Internalism and Externalism in Semantics and Epistemology*. Oxford: Oxford University Press: 201–218.

Hempel, Carl G. (1945). "On the Nature of Mathematical Truth." *American Mathematical Monthly* 52(10): 543–556.

Hilbert, David. (1950). *Foundations of Geometry*. La Salle: Open Court.

Hirsch, Eli and Jared Warren. (2019). "Quantifier Variance." In Kusch (ed.), *Routledge Handbook of Philosophy of Relativism*. London: Routledge: 349–357.

Huemer, Michael. (2009). "Explanationist Aid for the Theory of Inductive Logic." *British Journal for the Philosophy of Science* 60(2): 345–375.

Jenkins, Carrie. (2008). *Grounding Concepts: An Empirical Basis for Arithmetical Knowledge*. Oxford: Oxford University Press.

Kaplan, David. (1989). "Demonstratives." In Almog, Petty, and Wettstein (eds.), *Themes from Kaplan*. Oxford: Oxford University Press: 481–564.

Keynes, John Maynard. (1921). *A Treatise on Probability*. London: Macmillan.

Kitcher, Philip. (1984). *The Nature of Mathematical Knowledge*. Oxford: Oxford University Press.

Kripke, Saul A. (1980). *Naming and Necessity*. Cambridge, MA: Harvard University Press.

Leite, Adam. (2011). "Austin, Dreams, and Scepticism." In Gustafsson and Sørli (eds.), *The Philosophy of J.L. Austin*. Oxford: Oxford University Press: 78–113.

Maher, Patrick. (2006). "The Concept of Inductive Probability." *Erkenntnis* 65: 185–206.

Malmgren, Anna-Sara. (2006). "Is There A Priori Knowledge by Testimony?" *Philosophical Review* 115(2): 199–241.

Malmgren, Anna-Sara. (2013). "A Priori Testimony Revisited." In Casullo and Thurow (eds.), *The A Priori in Philosophy*. Oxford: Oxford University Press: 158–185.

Mares, Edwin. (2011). *A Priori*. Ithaca: McGill-Queen's University Press.

Maudlin, Tim. (2005). "The Tale of Quantum Logic." In Ben-Menahem (ed.), *Hilary Putnam*. Cambridge: Cambridge University Press: 156–187.

Maudlin, Tim. (2007). *The Metaphysics Within Physics*. Oxford: Oxford University Press.

Maudlin, Tim. (2012). *Philosophy of Physics: Space and Time*. Princeton: Princeton University Press.

Nozick, Robert. (1981). *Philosophical Explanations*. Cambridge, MA: Harvard University Press.

Peacocke, Christopher. (1992). *A Study of Concepts*. Cambridge, MA: The MIT Press.

Peacocke, Christopher. (2000). "Explaining the A Priori: The Programme of Moderate Rationalism." In Paul Boghossian and Christopher Peacocke (eds.), *New Essays on the A Priori*. Oxford: Oxford University Press: 255–285.

Plantinga, Alvin. (1993). *Warrant and Proper Function*. New York: Oxford University Press.

Poincaré, Henri. (1905). *Science and Hypothesis*. London: Scott.

Pollock, John L. (1987). "Defeasible Reasoning." *Cognitive Science* 11: 481–518.

Price, Henry H. (1940). *Hume's Theory of the External World*. Oxford: Clarendon Press.

Prior, Arthur N. (1960). "The Runabout Inference Ticket." *Analysis* 21: 2.

Putnam, Hilary. (1968). "Is Logic Empirical?" In Cohen and Wartofsky (eds.), *Boston Studies in the Philosophy of Science* Vol. 5. Dordrecht: Reidel: 216–241.

Putnam, Hilary. (1976). "'Two Dogmas' Revisited." In Ryle (ed.), *Contemporary Aspects of Philosophy*. Stocksfield: Oriel Press: 202–213.

Putnam, Hilary. (2005). "A Philosopher Looks at Quantum Mechanics (Again)." *British Journal for the Philosophy of Science* 56(4): 615–634.

Quine, Willard V. (1951). "Two Dogmas of Empiricism." *Philosophical Review* 60(1): 20–43.

Quine, W. V. (1960). *Word and Object*. Cambridge, MA: The MIT Press.

Quine. W. V. (1970). *Philosophy of Logic*. Englewood Cliffs: Prentice Hall.

Reichenbach, Hans. (1951). *The Rise of Scientific Philosophy*. Berkeley: University of California Press.

Russell, Bertrand. (1912). *The Problems of Philosophy*. London: Williams & Norgate.

Schiffer, Stephen. (2003). *The Things We Mean*. Oxford: Oxford University Press.

Schleidt, Wolfgang, Michael D. Shalter, and Humberto Moura-Neto. (2011). "The Hawk/Goose Story: The Classical Ethological Experiments of Lorenz and Timbergen, Revisited." *Journal of Comparative Psychology* 125(2): 121–133.

Shope, Robert K. (1983). *The Analysis of Knowing: A Decade of Research*. Princeton: Princeton University Press.

Sidelle, Alan. (1989). *Necessity, Essence, and Individuation: A Defense of Conventionalism*. Ithaca: Cornell University Press.

Sider, Theodore. (2011). *Writing the Book of the World*. Oxford: Oxford University Press.

Sklar, Lawrence. (1974). *Space, Time, and Spacetime*. Berkeley: University of California Press.

Sosa, Ernest. (1996). "Rational Intuition: Bealer on its Nature and Epistemic Status." *Philosophical Studies* 81: 151–162.

Turri, John. (2011). "Contingent A Priori Knowledge." *Philosophy and Phenomenological Research* 83(2): 327–344.

Warren, Jared. (2015a). "Conventionalism, Consistency, and Consistency Sentences." *Synthese* 192(5): 1351–1371.

Warren, Jared. (2015b). "Talking with Tonkers." *Philosophers' Imprint* 15(24): 1–24.

Warren, Jared. (2016). "Internal and External Questions Revisited." *Journal of Philosophy* 113(4): 177–209.

Warren, Jared. (2017). "Epistemology versus Non-Causal Realism." *Synthese* 194(5): 1643–1662.

Warren, Jared. (2018). "Change of Logic, Change of Meaning." *Philosophy and Phenomenological Research* 96(2): 421–442.

Warren, Jared. (2020). *Shadows of Syntax: Revitalizing Logical and Mathematical Conventionalism*. New York: Oxford University Press.

Warren, Jared. (2021). "Defending Understanding-Assent Links." *Synthese* 199(3–4): 9219–9236.

Warren, Jared. (forthcoming). "Inferentialism, Conventionalism, and *A Posteriori* Necessity." *Journal of Philosophy*.

Weatherson, Brian. (2012). "Induction and Supposition." *The Reasoner* 6: 78–80.

Williamson, Jon. (2010). *In Defence of Objective Bayesianism*. Oxford: Oxford University Press.

Williamson, Timothy. (1986). "The Contingent A Priori: Has it Anything to Do with Indexicals?" *Analysis* 46(3): 113–117.

Williamson, Timothy. (2000). *Knowledge and its Limits*. Oxford: Oxford University Press.

Williamson, Timothy. (2007). *The Philosophy of Philosophy.* Oxford: Blackwell.

Williamson, Timothy. (2013). "How Deep is the Distinction between A Priori and A Posteriori Knowledge?" In Casullo and Thurow (eds.), *The A Priori in Philosophy.* Oxford: Oxford University Press: 291–312.

Williamson, Timothy. (2016). "Knowing by Imagining." In Kind and Kung (eds.), *Knowledge through Imagination.* Oxford: Oxford University Press: 113–123.

Williamson, Timothy. (2020a). "Reply to Boghossian on Intuition, Understanding, and the A Priori." In Boghossian and Williamson, *Debating the A Priori.* Oxford: Oxford University Press: 208–213.

Williamson, Timothy. (2020b). "Reply to Boghossian on the Distinction between the A Priori and the A Posteriori." In Boghossian and Williamson, *Debating the A Priori.* Oxford: Oxford University Press: 156–167.

Wittgenstein, Ludwig. (1929). "Some Remarks on Logical Form." *Proceedings of the Aristotelian Society, Supplementary Volumes* 9: 162–171.

Wittgenstein, Ludwig. (1956). *Remarks on the Foundations of Mathematics.* New York: Macmillan.

Wittgenstein, Ludwig. (1974). *Philosophical Grammar.* Oxford: Basil Blackwell.

Wright, Crispin. (1986). "Inventing Logical Necessity." In Jeremy Butterfield (ed.), Language, Mind & Logic. Cambridge University Press: Cambridge: 187-209.

Wright, Crispin. (2006). "Inventing Logical Necessity." In Butterfield (ed.), *Language, Mind, & Logic.* Cambridge: Cambridge University Press: 187–209.

Acknowledgments

My thanks to:

Stephen Hetherington for the opportunity.

The participants in my spring 2021 seminar on core topics in philosophy and the fall 2021 Stanford philosophy proseminar (co-taught with John Etchemendy) where versions of what became Sections 2 and 4 were read and discussed.

Grace Tang for helping me through the crisis mentioned in the preface and for quarantine, with thoughts about nearby possible worlds.

Rosa Cao, Yu Guo, Eli Hirsch, Penn Lawrence, and Douglas Stalker for written comments on and discussion of a pre-submission draft, leading to numerous improvements.

Sharon Berry, Tom Donaldson, Zeynep Soysal, and Dan Waxman for discussion of a complete, pre-submission draft at a January 28, 2022 meeting of our global semi-regular reading and presentation group.

Two referees for Cambridge University Press for helpful and encouraging comments on the initially submitted draft leading to further philosophical and stylistic improvements (I hope).

Tianlin Meng Walsh for answering my questions about the dedication.

Darren Bradley and Douglas Stalker for comments on some additions made between initial and final submission.

To all rōnin philosophers.

Cambridge Elements

Epistemology

Stephen Hetherington
University of New South Wales, Sydney

Stephen Hetherington is Professor Emeritus of Philosophy at the University of New South Wales, Sydney. He is the author of numerous books including *Knowledge and the Gettier Problem* (Cambridge University Press, 2016), and *What Is Epistemology?* (Polity, 2019), and is the editor of, most recently, *Knowledge in Contemporary Epistemology* (with Markos Valaris: Bloomsbury, 2019), and *What the Ancients Offer to Contemporary Epistemology* (with Nicholas D. Smith: Routledge, 2020). He was the Editor-in-Chief of the *Australasian Journal of Philosophy* from 2013 until 2022.

About the Series

This Elements series seeks to cover all aspects of a rapidly evolving field including emerging and evolving topics such as these: fallibilism; knowing-how; self-knowledge; knowledge of morality; knowledge and injustice; formal epistemology; knowledge and religion; scientific knowledge; collective epistemology; applied epistemology; virtue epistemology; wisdom. The series will demonstrate the liveliness and diversity of the field, pointing also to new areas of investigation.

Cambridge Elements ☰

Epistemology

Elements in the Series

Printed in the United States
by Baker & Taylor Publisher Services